EEC and the Third World: A Survey 1

edited by Christopher Stevens

HODDER AND STOUGHTON
LONDON SYDNEY AUCKLAND TORONTO

in association with the Overseas Development Institute
and the Institute of Development Studies

British Library Cataloguing in Publication data

EEC and the Third World
  1. Underdeveloped areas – Foreign economic
relations
  2. European Economic Community countries –
Foreign economic relations
  I. Stevens, Christopher, *1948*–
  II. Overseas Development Institute III. Institute of
Development Studies
  382.1′094   HF1413

ISBN 0 340 26502 7

First published 1981

Represented in West Africa by Nigeria Publishers Services Ltd,
P. O. Box 62, Ibadan, Nigeria

Represented in East Africa by K. W. Martin, P. O. Box 30583,
Nairobi, Kenya

Printed in Great Britain for Hodder and Stoughton Educational,
a division of Hodder and Stoughton Ltd,
Mill Road, Dunton Green, Sevenoaks, Kent,
by Richard Clay (The Chaucer Press) Ltd, Bungay, Suffolk

Contents

Editorial Board

About the Contributors

David Birch was a Visiting Fellow at the Science Policy Research Unit, University of Sussex, during the preparation of this article, and is currently a lecturer at Griffiths University, Brisbane, Australia.

Kurt Hoffman is a Research Fellow at the Science Policy Research Unit, University of Sussex.

Adrian Hewitt is a Research Officer at the Overseas Development Institute, London.

Tony Killick is a Research Officer at the Overseas Development Institute, London.

Philip Mishalani is a doctoral research student at the Institute of Development Studies, Sussex.

Professor Peter R. Odell is Director of the Economic Geography Institute, Erasmus University, Rotterdam.

Annette Robert is a consultant in international relations and development, based in The Hague.

E. Verreydt is a researcher at the Centre of Mathematical Economics and Econometrics, Université Libre de Bruxelles.

Professor Jean Waelbroeck is Director of the Centre of Mathematical Economics and Econometrics, Université Libre de Bruxelles.

Ann Weston is a Research Officer at the Overseas Development Institute, London.

Addresses:

Overseas Development Institute,
10—11 Percy Street,
London WIP OJB

The Institute of Development Studies
at the University of Sussex,
Falmer,
Brighton, BN1 9RE

A note on EEC Units of Account

The EEC uses a variety of units to express values. The most commonly used in the context of trade and aid flows are the European Currency Unit (Ecu) established in December 1978 for use in the European Monetary Co-operation Fund, and the European Unit of Account (Eua) expressing the aid provisions of the Lomé Convention. Both units are based on a basket of European currencies, which is currently the same for both and comprises the sum of the following amounts:

German mark	0.828
Pound sterling	0.0885
French franc	1.15
Italian lira	109
Dutch guilder	0.286
Belgian franc	3.66
Luxembourg franc	0.14
Danish krone	0.217
Irish pound	0.00759

Although the baskets are identical, the two units are not revalued at the same intervals and so at any one time they may have slightly different values in terms of other currencies.

List of Abbreviations

AASM	Associated African States and Madagascar
ACP	African, Caribbean and Pacific (signatories to the Lomé Conventions)
ASEAN	Association of South East Asian Nations
BSC	British Sugar Corporation
CAP	Common Agricultural Policy
CEC	Commission of the European Communities
CIEC	Conference on International Economic Cooperation
dc	developed country
DG	Directorate-General (of the CEC)
ECSC	European Coal and Steel Community
EDF	European Development Fund
EEC	European Economic Community
EIB	European Investment Bank
FAC	Food Aid Convention
GATT	General Agreement on Tariffs and Trade
GSP	Generalised System of Preferences
IBRD	International Bank for Reconstruction and Development
ILO	International Labour Office
IMF	International Monetary Fund
IWA	International Wheat Agreement
ldc	developing country
MFA	Multifibre Agreement
mfn	most favoured nation
MTN	Multilateral Trade Negotiations
oda	official development assistance
OECD	Organisation for Economic Cooperation and Development
OPEC	Oil Producing and Exporting Countries
QR	Quantity Restriction
SDR	Special Drawing Rights
t.o.e.	tonnes of oil equivalent
VER	Voluntary Export Restraint

Editorial Policy

The Survey will provide an annual record and commentary of major developments in the European Community's economic relations with the Third World. Its audience will include policy makers, opinion formers and academics in the nine member countries and the Commission, and in North America and the Third World. Its underlying philosophy is that the EEC and the Third World have mutual interests. Neither harmony nor conflict of such interests is regarded as inevitable.

The Editorial Board is responsible for determining that this work should be presented to the public, but individual members of the Board are not responsible for statements of fact and expressions of opinion contained therein.

Foreword

This is the first of an annual series of *Surveys* which will review and comment upon major developments in the EEC's economic relations with the Third World. It aims to fill a major gap by pulling together the many strands of EEC (and where relevant member state) policies and actions that affect the Third World, and to bring to this assessment the weight of research being undertaken in European centres and elsewhere. It is, of course, highly selective; the aim is not to produce a voluminous yearbook of events, but to survey the state of EEC-Third World relations at a regular interval, focussing on key trends and events. The topics covered by the *Survey* will vary from year to year according to the Editorial Board's view of the most important developments. Two features, however, will remain the same in subsequent issues. First, the tables in the Statistical Appendix have been selected to illustrate key features of EEC-Third World links, and will be updated annually. Second, to make the *Survey* authoritative and brief the present pattern of authorship will be retained, with expert contributions ranging between 1,000 words and a full chapter combined with an active editorial involvement to ensure that the *Survey* does not become a loose collection of articles but remains a well-rounded commentary and record.

The extensive research and editorial work required for this first issue has only been made possible by the generous support of the Ford Foundation, the Institute of Development Studies, the Noel Buxton Trust and the Shell Grants Committee.

London
August 1980

1

The Search for Coherence

The dilemma facing the EEC in its relations with the Third World was neatly illustrated by *The Sunday Times* of 17 February 1980. On the centre page, in a review of the Brandt Report, which it described as 'The most important event this year', it boldly proclaimed that 'The world economy is breaking down . . . Bridging the gap between rich and poor is not only humane: it opens up a potential market of 2,000 million poor people. Nothing else will solve the North's problem of over-capacity, or ensure survival for the South.' Yet the same issue carried another story, with a very different message. It began 'The [UK] government is about to announce further cuts in overseas aid . . .'

The conflict between the views that North–South relations present an opportunity for mutual benefit, and that they are a source of mutual discord is a conflict between the short and the long-term, between the interests of the wider community and particular sections within it, and between blocs of states taken as a whole, and individual member countries. These tensions are not limited to the UK. The EEC is becoming increasingly concerned about the coherence of its multifarious policies, with a growing awareness that some policies contradict others. The Community's bold self-perception of its role in North–South affairs is encapsulated in a communication from the Commission to the Council of May 1980 regarding the forthcoming Global Negotiations.

the Community must demonstrate the political importance it attaches to the relaunching of the North–South Dialogue and must translate into practical terms the direct participation of its political leaders in the process of discussions between industrialised and developing countries. It is to the Community that the latter are looking for an initiative; it is the Community that is already the best-placed interlocutor of the developing countries within the United Nations, and lastly it is the Community that has been able to indicate the path of change in its relations with the developing countries at a regional level.[1]

This view of the EEC's centrality to North–South issues contrasts starkly with the communiqué of the Venice Western economic summit only a month later which bluntly declared that 'The democratic industrialised countries cannot alone carry the responsibility of aid and other different contributions to developing countries: it must be equitably shared by oil exporting countries and the industrialised Communist countries.'

These conflicts are perennial, but they were particularly visible in the EEC's relations with the Third World in 1979/80, and will remain so in 1980/81. An extra twist was added in 1979/80 because the Commissioners' terms of office were drawing to a close. The Commissioners' recent actions on North–South topics, as in other spheres, have to be viewed against this background of personal and political uncertainty. The whole issue of trade protectionism – whether Third World exports of manufactured goods are a 'problem' for the EEC, or an opportunity – moves closer to the centre of the political stage each year. 1979/80 saw the conclusion of GATT's Tokyo Round of tariff cuts; 1980/81 will see the re-negotiation of the Multifibre Agreement which controls Third World exports of textiles and clothing. On the agricultural front, 1979/80 saw the collapse of negotiations on the international wheat agreement, the attempted grain embargo on the USSR, a continuation of attempts to curb the EEC's common agricultural policy, and the failure to come to terms with a new sugar beet régime. All these issues have profound implications for developing countries. The oil price rises of 1979/80 have dominated public attention on non-agricultural, raw materials questions, but the year also witnessed growing concern on the part of the EEC for the long-term security of its mineral supplies, principally in Africa. This concern led it to attempt, during the negotiations for the second Lomé Convention, to persuade its Third World partners to agree to innovations that would facilitate mineral exploration by the private mining companies.

This *Survey* deals with all those problems. The four following chapters record the key events of 1979/80, analyse the most important issues linking the EEC and the Third World, and forecast the likely trend of events. Two of the chapters are primarily concerned with EEC *policies* (Lomé, other regional agreements, and the impact of enlargement); and two are primarily concerned with EEC *interests* (in the fields of industry and energy). Select statistical and documentary appendices provide further evidence of the nature and trend of EEC-Third World relations. The purpose of this first chapter is to draw out some of the conclusions and forecasts of the *Survey*, and to place the more specific chapters that follow in their wider context.

Brandt underscores mutual interests

The event to claim most public attention in this "wider context" of 1980 was the publication of the report of the Brandt Commission (technically, the Independent Commission on International Development Issues). The Commission comprised 18 distinguished politicians and economists from the West and the South (but not the East), and was essentially a political initiative to generate a momentum to North–South issues and to forge a new kind of development relationship based on the mutual interests of the two sides. Few of the Commission's proposals are new. Their importance derives not from their originality, but from the fact that a sceptical group of seasoned practitioners have accepted that they are valid, feasible and, above all, necessary. By the same token, the Commission's success depends almost entirely on whether or not it really does succeed in establishing a new momentum.

Its proposals, which are outlined in the Box, fall into two groups: the first is a wide-ranging programme of priorities for the next two decades covering changes in the international economy and its institution, a compact between energy consumers and producers, an improvement in the conditions of trade in commodities and manufactures, and reform of the world monetary system and the structure of development finance. Second, the Commission has proposed an emergency programme for 1980–85 including a large-scale transfer of resources to ldcs, an international energy strategy, a global food programme, and the first steps to reform the international economic system.

The Report has been welcomed in general terms by most of the EEC member states, but the reservations have far outweighed the commitments to positive action. According to some sources two-thirds of the Venice summit of seven Western leaders (June 22–23 1980) was devoted to discussion of North–South issues, and the 1981 Western economic summit in Canada is expected to be devoted entirely to these issues. Optimists may be inclined to give more weight to this indication of concern for the importance of North–South topics than to the actual content of the communiqué that resulted. While it welcomed the Brandt Report and made a pledge 'to review aid policies and procedures and other contributions to developing countries and to report back . . . to the next summit', there were no firm commitments. Furthermore, the communique made very clear that the leaders considered 'the key to success in resolving the major economic challenges which the world faces', not to be North–South relations but the need 'to achieve and maintain a balance between energy supply and demand'.

Key Recommendations of the Brandt Commission

Development Finance & Institutions

- At least $400 million extra aid annually for the next 20 years for the low income ldcs, to be financed by a mandatory international system of revenue mobilisation (perhaps a progressive tax), and an increase in the industrialised countries' official aid to 0.7 %, GNP by 1985, and 1 % by 2000.
- Greater access to concessionary and commercial finance (on better terms) for middle- and higher-income ldcs, to be achieved *inter alia* by greater involvement of public institutions in lending, a doubling of IBRD's loan/capital ratio, and use of IMF's gold as loan collateral.
- Institutional reforms, possibly including increased ldc participation in the IMF and IBRD, and the creation of a World Development Fund with universal membership and broad management sharing, to emphasise programme lending.

Energy

- A guarantee by oil producers to maintain production levels and by oil consumers to meet conservation targets and to maintain the value and accessibility of the unit of payment.

- In the longer run, a multilateral financing facility for developing ldc energy resources.

Food

- Additional aid of $8,000 million annually for 20 years to agricultural development, coupled with domestic measures in ldcs to boost agriculture, notably land reform.
- Commodity agreements to stabilise world food supply and prices, and a reduction of agricultural protectionism in the North.
- The provision of emergency food supplies, including a food financing facility of $200 million annually to keep short-term cereal availability close to long-term trends.

Restructuring the International Economy

- A new international monetary system founded on more stable exchange rates, greater symmetry between the responsibilities of surplus and deficit countries for adjusting to balance of payments disequilibria, and an orderly expansion of world liquidity, with SDRs becoming the principal reserve asset and being distributed in favour of ldcs bearing the greatest adjustment burdens. As a step in this direction, the IMF should be more flexible in its attitude towards ldc balance of payments problems.

- Removal by the North of protectionist barriers to the processed exports of the South, the abolition of restrictive business practices, and finance to facilitate Southern processing and marketing.

- A Common Fund with sufficient resources to enable effective inter-national commodity agreements to be formed in order to stabilise commodity prices.

Note

The Brandt Report has been published as *North-South: A Programme for Survival* (Pan Books, 1980)

If the Venice communiqué provides little cause to comfort advocates of a Brandt-style action programme, the EEC Commission's preparatory documents for the eleventh special session of the UN provide a glimmer of hope. The special session, scheduled for 25 August – 5 September 1980, was conceived to adopt the international strategy for the third United Nations Development Decade, and to discuss the framework and agenda for the North–South Global Negotiations which are due to resume in January 1981. A Communication by the Commission to the Council of May 1980 argued that 'a broader international effort is still needed; clearly, there must be a firm commitment from the industrialised countries as a whole . . .'. And although it went on to reiterate the concern expressed at Venice and elsewhere that the oil producers must be induced to play a major role, it also pressed the EEC to 'help promote' the Brandt Commission's emergency programme which it described as 'well calculated to deal with the most urgent problems of the current situation and the tasks immediately before us.' And there is other documentary evidence of Commission pressure for the EEC to declare that it is prepared to reach the aid target of 0.7% of GNP 'in the course of the decade'.

Clearly such views are not accepted unanimously in the governments of the Nine. However, the Commission's Communications are important even if they are not immediately accepted by the Council, since they indicate the drift of thinking in a powerful Community institution, which, being permanent, can always come back to fight another day. This being the case, one of the most interesting features of the May Communication to Council is the light it shines on the Commission's conception of the key areas for action. Under the heading 'What is to be gained by further dialogue?' it argues:

The collective aims which the Community should set for a reactivated dialogue are of three kinds:

(i) Countering the threat of deep and widespread recession facing the economies of both North and South: there are clear risks to the international economic system and world peace itself in current developments; these risks could become aggravated with the strangulation of the poorest developing countries and cessation of the growth process in middle-income developing countries.

(ii) Easing world hunger: insecurity of food supplies at world level is beyond doubt the least tolerable of all forms of uncertainty, and it is an absolute moral imperative for the international community to reduce this insecurity.

(iii) Organising the transition to a less oil-dependent world economy: the foreseeable imbalance between the oil supplies and potential demand over the next few years places a serious question mark over the chances of continuing the growth and development process. The second 'oil crisis' and the continuing tremors it has set up show that disorderly escalation of oil prices and uncertainties of supply will remain a problem until some way is found of establishing comprehensive cooperation between energy producers and consumers.[2]

This chapter relates to all three of these concerns.

Protectionism

At the heart of the first of the three is the debate over protectionism. The year 1979/80 began on a liberal note with the completion of the long-drawn out GATT 'Tokyo Round' of multilateral trade negotiations (MTN). When the MTNs were formally wound up in November 1979 considerable ill-feeling was expressed by developing countries which felt that their interests had been overlooked. The results of the MTNs in relation to formal constraints on trade are quite impressive. Tariffs on industrial products have been reduced by an average of 38% or 33% (depending on the weighting used). However, there are drawbacks. First, the tariff reductions on smaller industrial products of particular interest to developing countries have been rather less; one estimate gives an average of 37% or 26% (depending on the weighting used).[3] Second, any generalised reduction of tariffs reduces the benefit that developing countries derive from the myriad of preferential arrangements accorded them by the industrialised countries (those relating to the EEC are described in Chapter 4). Third, and most important, tariffs are not the critical constraint on exports of a number of products of particular importance to developing countries. The Tokyo Round does nothing to ease the restrictions imposed by the Multifibre Agreement, for example. One major item left unfinished in November 1979 concerns the imposition of import controls under GATT. Under existing arrangements, importing countries may take action under Article 19 to impose 'emergency safeguard measures' if a domestic industry is adversely affected by a 'rapid' and 'damaging' rise in imports. The spread of protectionist sentiment has increased the pressure on some industrialised country governments to impose such import control. But they have found Article 19 difficult to use in practice because it requires any import controls that are imposed to be applied across-the-board to all sources of supply. The EEC in particular has argued for a selective safeguards clause that would permit controls to be imposed against the exports of individual countries. The developing countries fear that they would feel the brunt of such selective safeguards. There is a view that states are inhibited from invoking Article 19 for fear of retaliation by strong trading partners. Selectivity would allow controls to be specially tailored so that they fall only on exporting countries that are unable to retaliate effectively, a category that includes many developing countries. The EEC attempted to gain acceptance for its proposed selective safeguards clause both during and after the Tokyo Round negotiations. It has so far failed, but has indicated in word and deed that it intends unilaterally to use Article 19 selectively as it sees fit.

Verreydt and Waelbroeck forecast in Chapter 2, that despite the growing pressure for protectionism, the EEC as a Community will not erect wideranging restrictions on imports from developing countries, if only because the Community's internal dynamic works on the whole in favour of free trade. Similarly, the EEC institutions do not have the power to initiate positive adjustment with a 'Japan Inc', or French 'Contrat de Programme' style of industrial planning. Attempts to initiate such policies tend to stir up national jealousies which doom them to failure.

Thus the EEC tends to react in an ad hoc fashion to the pressures exerted upon it, rather than initiate a wideranging structure of either protection or positive adjustment. The strength of these pressures need not be closely related to the underlying strength of the lobbyists' case. Chapter 2 reiterates the points made in numerous studies that imports from developing countries are not a major cause of unemployment (technical change is overwhelmingly more important), and that even supposedly hard-hit industries such as textiles have within them sub-sectors that are perfectly able to compete with all-comers: German industrial textiles and carpets in the Flanders 'carpet freeway' being two cases in point. The problem, of course, is that the uncompetitive sectors make much more noise than those that are competitive. Moreover, while developing countries' exports may not be a potent cause of un-employment, they are a more vulnerable target for lobbyists than are the other causes. The two sides of industry can more easily join in common cause against imports (which both oppose) than against technological advance (which management may favour). And it is generally more easy for governments to respond to pressure against developing country exports than against those of developed countries simply because the former are much weaker and have fewer opportunities for retaliation.

Thus, protectionist devices may be most expected in industries where countervailing pressure from domestic interests or from foreign countries would be weak, and least expected in cases where they would be strong. Waelbroeck and Verreydt do not anticipate that the EEC's recent actions in the steel sector under the Davignon Plan will develop into a fully fledged system of market and import controls along the lines of the common agricultural policy, since EEC steel users recognise that their interests would be adversely affected. Germany is the most important EEC exporter of metal products and it is therefore not surprising that German representatives have been pressing hard for a strong link between steel market regulation and rationalisation of output. Similarly, the authors do not expect protectionism in shipbuilding because the industry's consumer, the world shipping industry, can easily manoeuvre around such controls. It is in the textile, clothing and footwear industries that protectionism is most likely to flourish. The EEC position at the forthcoming negotiations for the renewal of the Multifibre Agreement (MFA III) will be an important sign both for European interests and for those in the Third World. It will signal to EEC producers generally the degree to which their governments are determined to force them to adjust, or are willing to yield to pressure for protection. And it will influence investment decisions in the Third World. As the 'first sector of in-dustrialisation' textiles and clothing play a key role for ldc exporters of manufactured goods. The current Multifibre Agreement (MFA II) froze the geographic pattern of imports into the EEC by allocating the lion's share of quotas to the early starters. A restrictive MFA III will reinforce the belief in other ldcs that the road is now closed, and could encourage them to evolve into closed economies isolated from the world.

A portent of the EEC's position on MFA III emerged in mid-1980 when it was reported that the Community was drafting a standardised policy to cover textile imports from the African, Caribbean and Pacific (ACP) signatories of the Lomé Convention. As explained in Chapter 3, Lomé provides the ACP with duty free access to the EEC market for their industrial exports. Clothing and textiles form a minute but growing proportion of total ACP exports, and there has been evidence in the past of some arm twisting by the Commission and by certain member states to persuade ACP exporters to exercise 'restraint'. Now it appears that the EEC is planning to set formal quotas, in clear violation of the Lomé spirit.[4]

Food: mutual or conflicting interests?

The European Parliament, with the strong support of the Commissioner for Development, Claude Cheysson, devoted a significant part of its first year to considering the issue of 'Hunger in the World'. Parliament took up the issue after the Ottawa meeting of the World Food Council in September 1979, and resolved to consider four aspects: food production in developing countries, food aid, the international food market and external effects of the common agricultural policy (CAP). These topics absorbed the energies of four of its committees – development and cooperation, external affairs, political affairs, and agriculture – although the final resolution, debated at Parliament's September 1980 session, was drafted by the development and cooperation committee. This *Survey* went to press before the final version of the resolution had been agreed or debated in plenary. However, drafts of the resolution contained, in addition to the predictable references to the need to facilitate agricultural self-sufficiency in the developing countries, some bold references to the common agricultural policy and its effects on Third World agriculture. The European Parliament has few concrete powers. Like the Brandt Commission, therefore, the success of its deliberations will depend on the degree to which it provides a political impetus to further action. With the changeover of Commissioners, the prospects for such an impetus depend very much on Parliament continuing to give prominence to food issues. However, there are at least three food-related issues that will come to the fore in the near future independently of the Parliament's pressure. They are EEC food aid, the international grain trade, and EEC imports of commodities that are currently produced within the Community, or will be when its membership is increased to twelve.

EEC Food Aid: *pressure for reform mounts*

The EEC is a substantial donor of food aid. In 1979 it committed 720,500 tons of cereals (mainly wheat), 150,000 tons of dried skim milk and 45,000 tons of butteroil. International statistics on food aid are notoriously bad, but the cereals commitment represents around 8% of total world commitments. In addition, EEC member states have substantial bilateral cereals food aid programmes: 55% of EEC cereals aid is channelled through the Community programme, and 45% through member states' national programmes (dairy product food aid is channelled wholly through the Community programme). The EEC food aid programme has often been criticised for failings that are ostensibly administrative, but in reality have political roots. In its 1979 audit, the EEC Court of Auditors produced a catalogue of criticisms concerning the complexity of administration, the execution of budget appropriations, delays in planning and executing aid programmes, deficiencies in procedures for mobilising aid, mishaps affecting transport of aid and insufficient checks on the execution of aid projects and the use to which proceeds of sale are put.[5] Following this audit, the Court embarked upon a major study of the administration of the food aid programme scheduled to be published in the second half of 1980. The European Parliament's study of food aid in the context of 'Hunger in the World' was also critical of EEC efforts in a number of respects, and even the Economic and Social Committee has added its voice to the chorus of complaints. There are mixed views on the desirability of food aid. Critics have identified a number of ways in which food aid could potentially harm the recipient, and although none of these adverse consequences are inevitable and, in practice, are often avoided, the EEC's procedures make it harder than it need be to ensure that this happens.

Reform is therefore very likely to be on the agenda in 1981. Whether it will result in a change of practice is another matter. At the root of these problems is the desire of the member states to influence the allocation of food aid between the various states that request it, and their desire for the programme to serve both development and agricultural policy. As a result, the Council insists on approving all country allocations every year and on doing so not one by one but in a single bumper package. This means that the Community can give recipients no guarantee either of the continuity of supplies between years, or of the timeliness of their arrival. Moreover, responsibility for compiling and implementing the annual programme is split between the Commission directorates-general for development and for agriculture, and the agricultural intervention boards in the member states. The Court of Auditors has argued forcefully that 'this diffusion of powers is by its nature prejudicial to the administration of the aid programmes and of their finances'.[6]

International Wheat Agreement

On a different level, the international wheat agreement (IWA) and food aid convention (FAC) will be the subject of negotiations in 1981. The 1971 IWA attempts to influence world trade in wheat, the most important internationally traded grain. The FAC is its siamese twin, and is a commitment by the major donors to keep food aid in cereals above a specified minimum level. Both were due to expire in June 1978. From mid-1977 efforts were made in the context of the GATT multilateral trade negotiations to agree a new IWA with wider provisions including controls over prices and supplies, nationally held buffer stocks and possible extension to other grains. At the same time, talks began on a new FAC with a higher minimum food aid commitment. But the negotiations on a new IWA broke down in February 1979, largely because of a failure by the main exporters and importers to agree on the prices at which the food stocks would come into operation. The parties were close to agreement on a new FAC, but because of the siamese twin relationship when the IWA talks were suspended so were those on the FAC. In both cases, the 1971 accords were simply extended.

There followed a number of efforts to separate the two issues, and to establish a new FAC in advance of agreement on an IWA. This is an area where negotiating responsibility has been transferred from the EEC member states to the Commission. However, because there are divergent views among the Nine, and because grain trade issues are very important for all the member states, the Commission is normally given a very restricted negotiating mandate by the Council. There are two main areas of divergence among the Nine. The first is between the food exporters (most notably France) and the food importers (including UK). The second is over treatment of developing countries, with Holland and Denmark tending to be more flexible than UK, Germany and France. These two areas of divergence overlapped on the issue of separating the IWA and FAC. Immediately after the collapse of negotiations, the agreed EEC position was fairly strongly opposed to separation, partly because to do so might reduce pressure on the developing country importers to reach agreement on a new IWA. However, international pressure for separation slowly grew and before the end of the year both Canada and USA had come out in favour. The EEC then shifted its position too, and as a result a new FAC was initialled on 6 March 1980 and came into force on the following 1 July.

While the separation of the IWA and FAC was a political advance for the likely beneficiaries of food aid, the new FAC has a major flaw: it lasts only one year. Since its purpose is to ensure a basic minimum of food aid even in years of tight supply it should cover several years. The minimum annual food aid agreed is 7,592,000 tons, with the EEC committed to providing 21.7% of this total through Community and national programmes. The new minimum is significantly greater than the 4.2 million tons under the old FAC, but it is less than the quantity that has actually been committed in recent years. In 1978/79 cereal food aid commitments totalled 9.744 million tons, and in 1979/80 they were 8.996 million tons. The importance of the new FAC should be seen, therefore, in the political impetus it gives either to a permanent separation, or to getting the IWA negotiators back to the table. It is expected that in 1981, with the US presidential elections out of the way, talks on a new IWA will begin again in earnest. And, because of its one year life, the FAC will also have to be re-negotiated.

Sugar: the competition between beet and cane

Another agricultural agreement coming up for renegotiation with implications for EEC-Third World relations is the Community's sugar beet régime. In 1975 the EEC agreed a five year régime providing domestic beet producers with guaranteed market prices which are, in general, substantially higher than world levels, but only for a fixed quota of production. The 1975 régime was due to expire on June 30 1980, but the Nine could not agree on the level of quotas for the new quinquennium. At its June 1980 meeting, therefore, the Council of Ministers agreed that the existing régime should be extended for a further year and that the Commission should produce a fresh set of proposals. These are likely to be unveiled in Autumn 1980, and may well include higher quotas than were recommended in the first Commission proposals. This, in turn, raises the prospect that the EEC's commitment to import 1.3 million tons of cane sugar annually from the ACP and India may, in the words of the UK industrial consumers of sugar, 'wither on the vine'.

There are three levels of quotas. Farmers receive full price support on the quantity included in their 'A' quota. In addition, there is a 'B' quota on which a production levy is charged to help meet the cost of export subsidies for any surplus sugar. The levy is split between the farmers, 60%, and the processors, 40%. Finally, there is 'C' sugar. Any production over the A and B quota limits is treated as 'C' sugar: it receives no price support and must be sold on the world market for the going rate. The existence of these quotas is, in theory at least, an imperfection to be removed as soon as possible. They were included in the 1968 regime for a 'transitional period to make provisions for measures to limit production and promote regional specialisation'.[8] But when the regime was renewed in 1975, the Commission calculated that if the quotas were scrapped there would have to have been a cut in the support price of at least 25 % to keep production within the desired levels. Quotas were retained, therefore, but they were set at too high a level.

The world sugar market is characterised by cycles in which relatively long periods of low prices are separated by relatively short periods of high prices. When setting quota levels for a quinquennium the EEC has to make a judgment about the likely world price/production trend. In 1974/1975 world sugar production was unusually low and prices were therefore high. The EEC chose to believe that the high prices were at least partly due to a structural rather than a purely cyclical shortage. The Commission recommended that the quotas that had been in force since 1968 should be extended. But the Council of Ministers disregarded this recommendation and increased the quotas by one-quarter. The current negotiations for a renewed régime are taking place against a similar background of high world prices. Accordingly, there is pressure to maintain existing quotas. In evidence to a UK House of Lords select committee in 1980, the British Sugar Corporation (BSC) argued that demand on the world market would 'continue to exceed production for some years'.[9] However, the select committee disagreed with the conclusion the BSC drew from this that quota reductions might not be required. Instead, the committee argued that 'it is poor practice to make long-term policy in reaction to short-term events. This is what happened at the last production quota review in 1974 when the Community over-reacted to a short-term situation. The same mistake must be guarded against this time.'[10] But the BSC is not alone in its views. France, in particular, is believed to have argued a similar line in the Council of Ministers.

Although the world market is currently characterised by excess demand over supply, the same is not true of the EEC market. Since the mid-1970s production in the Nine has outstripped consumption and exports have increased as an outlet for excess domestic supply. Since most of this has been under the 'A' and 'B' quotas it has been subsidised. The

UK is one of only two EEC members that are not self-sufficient in beet sugar. It has traditionally obtained a significant proportion of its requirements from imports of cane sugar, mainly from the Commonwealth, and when it joined the EEC a condition of membership was that the interests of developing country sugar exporters be safeguarded. As a result the EEC in 1975 entered into an agreement with the sugar producing signatories of the Lomé Convention plus India to import annually some 1.3 million tons of cane sugar at a price within the range received by Community farmers. Although the UK is not the sole consumer of cane sugar – France imports and processes cane sugar from its départements d'outre mer (DOM) – some 95% of the cane sugar shipped to Europe under the Lomé sugar protocol is actually consumed in the UK. While the UK retains an interest in cane, the balance of supply (and hence of pressure on the government) has shifted in the years since entry into the EEC. The Lomé sugar protocol extends preferential arrangements to the developing country beneficiaries of the Commonwealth Sugar Agreement, but it excludes Australia which had a 350,000 ton quota under the Commonwealth régime. Furthermore, under the 1974/75 régime, Britain was allocated a quota for beet that was greatly in excess of its existing production level. In 1974/75 568,000 tons of white sugar equivalent, or 23% of total domestic consumption, was supplied from domestic beet. But Britain's 'A' quota was set at 1,040,000 tons of white sugar, together with a 'B' quota of 286,000 tons. In the light of this, the British Sugar Corporation launched a £150 million expansion plan pegged to a production and marketing objective of 1.25 million tons. It has therefore reacted very strongly against the Commission proposals for the new quinquennium which would have reduced the UK's 'A' and 'B' quota to just over 1 million tons.

The outcome of the EEC's internal wranglings over the level of beet quotas has important implications for the cane producers. But the link is an indirect one, and involves the Tate and Lyle company which is the sole UK-based refiner of cane sugar. In evidence to a UK House of Lords select committee in 1979, the Commonwealth Sugar Exporters' Association stated unambiguously that the ACP sugar industries have 'a direct and vital interest in the maintenance of a viable refining industry in the United Kingdom which is their principal market'.[11] Tate and Lyle argue that because of the way the beet price support system operates excess beet production in the EEC threatens the continued viability of their cane refining activities. EEC price support applies to the processed product (white and raw sugar) not to the farmgate product (beet or cane). The sugar régime consequently stipulates the proportion of the intervention price that shall accrue to the farmer, and the margin available to the processor. The beet processor's margin has been set at a level much higher than that available to cane refiners, and the difference is quite striking: the BSC margin on the 1978/1979 crop was £13 per ton against £2 per ton for Tate and Lyle. Consequently in a situation of excess supply over demand (such as currently applies in UK) the BSC has scope to cut margins to increase its market share.

The Lomé sugar protocol is of 'indefinite duration'. Although it contains the provision that after five years it can be denounced with two years notice, the EEC has stated that this let-out clause was included purely for reasons of 'juridical security'. The new Lomé Convention, signed in October 1979, and described in detail in Chapter 3, maintains the original protocol (plus subsequent annexures). Yet there is a danger not that the protocol will be axed but that it will 'wither on the vine'. If the UK cane refining industry collapses, who will process the ACP sugar? There are provisions for the Commission to step in as a 'buyer of last resort', but it is not clear what it could do with the raw sugar. It could send some to beet refineries for processing, but this solution suffers from several severe practical and political drawbacks. Or it could re-export the raw sugar onto the world market. But then it would compete with the ACP's other exports. There already exists widespread resentment among sugar producers at the EEC's activities as an exporter onto the world market. Australia and Brazil have both made complaints to GATT over alleged dumping by the EEC. The UK House of Lords select committee has concluded that 'The Community's policy towards other exporters to the world sugar market appears to be one of selfishness and cynicism . . . '.[12]

As part of its efforts to achieve a degree of coherence in its Third World tasks, the Commission has drawn attention to what it sees as 'inconsistencies' between sugar aid and trade policies. In an information document in 1979, it argued that it was inconsistent to promote sugar development projects in the ACP on the one hand, and on the other to restrict the volume of ACP sugar exports entitled to benefit from the Lomé preferences. Since the EEC 'cannot contemplate any increase whatsoever in the total quota,' the Commission proposed that 'there should be full coordination of all on-going or projected schemes which the Member States or indeed, the Community (EDF, EIB) might support directly or indirectly. The attention of other financing bodies (World Bank, African Development Bank, etc.) is to be drawn to the Commission's conclusions.'[13] This document was based on an internal Commission report of November 1978 which was, in turn, prompted by a Zambian request to be covered by the Lomé sugar protocol. The internal report was not drafted in the directorate-general for agriculture as might be supposed from its general thrust, but in the directorate-general for development following an initiative at the highest level. And it extended its case beyond sugar, and argued that similar consultations should be organised in all sectors where a significant export growth from developing countries, and from the ACP in particular, might conceivably create serious problems of profitability and disturbances on the world or community market.

In other words, the Commission was proposing that both EEC and other donors' aid be tailored to ensure that it did not support schemes that would increase developing country exports in any way that might *conceivably* disrupt the Community market. This proposal met strong resistance from EEC industrial exporters, and was dropped in its original form. However, the basic idea has not been dropped, and the Commission is now trying to establish an information system about member states' exports of sugar technology and expertise. A further twist to the sugar tangle at the time of writing, was linked to Zimbabwe's application to adhere to the Lomé Convention and its sugar protocol. Commission officials spent much of the summer 1980 devising a means to accommodate three incompatibles: Zimbabwe's request for a sugar quota, the Community's desire not to increase the global quota, and the desire of the other signatories that their existing quotas should not be cut to make room.

EEC Enlargement and Third World Exports

Sugar is a sensitive issue because it is a commodity in which European and developing countries compete. It is in an unusual position because the protection afforded to European farmers by the common agricultural policy (CAP) is sufficiently watertight to rule out effective competition by developing countries on most products that can be grown in Europe. Even so, there are other agricultural exports from the Third World besides sugar that have found a niche in the interstices of the CAP, usually because domestic EEC production cannot fully supply the market, or can do so only at certain times of the year. Chapter 4 describes the intricate pattern of the EEC's trading links with developing countries and describes how the carefully and tightly drawn concessions on CAP products have been achieved through long and hard bargaining. The chapter goes on to explain how these concessions may be put at risk when Greece, Spain and Portugal join the Community.

Third World exporters to the EEC face increased competition from the new entrants not just for their agricultural products but also for industrial goods and for their migrant labour. Chapter 4 examines all three sets of commodities. But the most severe disruption is likely to be felt by the Maghreb's agricultural exports, and to be occasioned by Spanish entry. In a nutshell, enlargement will increase the EEC's domestic supply of certain CAP products relative to demand and will squeeze out Third World exports.

The original timetable was for Greece to become the EEC's tenth member in January 1981, and for Spain and Portugal to follow suit in 1983. But by mid-1980 the EEC was beginning to worry aloud about the impact of enlargement upon the Community's *internal* arrangements (let alone its relations with third parties), and it seemed likely that serious talks on Spanish and Portuguese membership would be stalled at least until after the French presidential elections of summer 1981. When they do begin, it is important that the interests of developing countries are given due weight. In an initial report in March 1980 on the problems associated with Spanish entry, the Commission confirmed that some developing countries would be adversely affected, and argued that measures were needed to recompense them, but it did not specify what measures would be adequate.

The Commission report identifies olive oil and vegetable fats, fruit and vegetables, and wine as the most problematic commodities from an internal EEC viewpoint. They are also among the most vulnerable Third World exports. Spain's farmers will add more to the EEC's supply of olive oil than its consumers will add to demand. As a result, the Commission forecasts a 200,000 tonne olive oil surplus. Its proposed solution is that competing vegetable oils be taxed to make them more expensive relative to olive oil and in that way to increase demand. Naturally, this is a controversial proposal, and when the hard bargaining begins it may prove expedient to reduce olive oil supply by cutting imports. This would hit Tunisia and Morocco, both of which are major exporters to the EEC. A similar situation obtains with wine. The problem is similar (Spanish entry will swell the EEC's wine lake by some 15%) as is the Commission's proposal (to change relative tax levels and so increase demand for wine at the expense of competing beverages). This will not be popular, and so wine imports may be curbed, which will principally affect Algeria and also Cyprus. The Mediterranean and other developing countries currently supply the EEC at certain times of the year with a wide range of fruit and vegetables. Tomatoes and citrus fruits are among the products most vulnerable to Spanish entry. The Commission has proposed, for example, that Spanish production of tomatoes be accommodated by a cut in Northern European hothouse production, but this is likely to be opposed in the countries affected.

The adverse impact of enlargement is not restricted to the Mediterranean, to Spanish entry or to agricultural products alone. Indonesia and Senegal, for example, as vegetable oil exporters will be affected by EEC policy changes on olive oil. Similarly Greece poses the main problem for Third World exporters of cotton and tobacco, and a wide range of countries, from the newly industrialising countries of Asia to Malta and Yugoslavia will be affected by the shift in the EEC's pattern of industrial production and trade following enlargement. Moreover, the impact may not be limited to trade. The Commission has suggested that the most severely affected developing countries be partially compensated by increased aid. If such an increase is not met by an expansion of the EEC's total aid budget it will, presumably, result in a reduction in the aid available for other developing countries.

Energy and Minerals

The EEC is concerned for the long-term security of its mineral supplies from the Third World, and Africa in particular. A Commission communication to Council of March 1979 referred to 'the alarming manner in which Africa in particular has lagged behind in mineral exploration over the past ten years . . .'[14] It went on to argue that in the context of the Lomé II negotiations an attempt should be made by the EEC 'to define on *a contractual basis* the details of the action to be taken in an area of mutual interest'.[15] It recommended three types of action: for public financing bodies (most notably the European Investment Bank – EIB) to act as a catalyst in attracting direct investment from European mining firms; for the EEC to conclude standard investment protection agreements with developing country governments; and for the Community to provide the private mining houses with financial guarantees against 'non-economic risks'. In the event, as Chapter 3 explains, these proposals were never formally put before the ACP in their entirety because the Nine could not agree among themselves. Instead, the new Lomé Convention contains references to increased aid for the energy and mining sectors, a second-cousin to the Stabex scheme for minerals, which is known variously as Minex or Sysmin, and a form of 'most favoured nation' treatment for investment codes whereby the ACP agree that they will tend to extend codes negotiated bilaterally with one EEC member state to the other Eight.

Despite the failure of the Commission to have its proposals translated into action, its perception of the EEC's mineral problem remains. So, too, does its perception of the solution. In essence this is that the private mining companies must be enticed back into the role they formerly played of discovering, developing and exploiting Africa's mineral resources. This underlying concept of the centrality of the mining companies to all stages of mineral exploitation has been strongly criticised.[16] Yet there is no evidence so far of a fundamental revision in Commission thinking. Since the second Lomé Convention failed to achieve the kind of changes the Commission believes necessary, the subject is likely to remain on the agenda in the coming years. The EEC concern is not that mineral supplies will dry up, but that the source of supply will increasingly shift away from Africa and other Third World countries that are relatively weak bargaining partners, towards North America and Australia which are in a much stronger position to demand concessions.

There is an exactly parallel conflict in the realm of energy supplies between the corporate interests of the companies on which European supplies depend (which tend to orientate them towards developed country ventures) and the broader interests of the EEC states (which want a wider geographical spread). In his opening section of chapter 5, Odell argues that the oil companies have failed to take a serious interest in very large petroliferous areas of the Third World because it is not in their interests to do so. He argues that 'this institutionalised dichotomy . . . appears to be the main barrier to the rapid geographical diversification of world oil reserves and the development of an enhanced supply potential'.

One of his proposed solutions is greatly increased official aid to energy projects. EEC aid to energy projects is expected to exceed Eua 800 million in 1980. In the third section of Chapter 5, Burch and Hoffman examine the nature and effects of this aid. Ironically in view of Odell's case, there is very little money for the oil sector. Instead, almost three-quarters of EEC energy aid so far under Lomé I has gone to hydroelectric power schemes, which is partly a reflection of the conventional pattern of funding adopted by other major aid agencies such as the World Bank. Under Lomé II, the EEC plans to increase its aid to alternative energy sources, which currently receive under 10% of the total. But 'alternative' does not necessarily mean 'appropriate'. There is a danger that energy aid may be too closely related to the exporting interests of the donor and too loosely related to the energy needs of the recipient.

One of the most prominent aspects of the current round of oil price rises is the question of recycling the oil producers' enormous balance of payments surplus. The conventional wisdom is that after the 1973–74 oil price rise, the banks played a key role in recycling and, moreover, that the developing countries were significant beneficiaries of their actions. The key question this time around seems, therefore, to be: can they do it again? Killick examines this conventional wisdom in the second section of Chapter 5 and concludes that it is ill founded. The banks did play a major role in recycling, but the developing countries were not significant beneficiaries. The conventional wisdom is based on two misperceptions. First, there is the problem that the term 'developing countries' includes an enormous variety of conditions ranging from the poorest states to those like Brazil and South Korea to which the term no longer fully applies. Much of the banks' lending was to a handful of states close to the upper income end of the developing country category. Second, it refers to gross not to net flows. The non-oil developing countries have been major depositors with the banks as well as major borrowers. When net flows are taken into account a very different picture emerges from that conventionally held. The poorest developing countries, far from being beneficiaries of recycling, have witnessed an outflow of funds.

Prospects are therefore bleak for financing the balance of payments deficits of the poorer developing countries following the current oil price rises. It is not simply a question of persuading the commercial banks to shoulder the burden again. Last time round, the poorer developing countries bore the brunt of the global adjustment needed to counterbalance the OPEC surplus, and had to cut back on imports. This time, the probability is that they will have to cut back even more. It has been observed that the Brandt Report has emerged at a singularly unpropitious time for the industrialised countries as recession begins to bite. But for the developing countries, the time has never been more urgent.

Notes

1   *Reactivation of the North-South Dialogue* com (80) 302 final (Brussels 29 May 1980) p. 4.
2   Com (80) 302 final (Brussels 29 May 1980) p. 1.
3   Cited in Bela Balassa 'The Tokyo Round and the Developing Countries' *Journal of World Trade Law* (vol. 14 No 2, March: April 1980) p. 98.
4   *Africa Economic Digest* (London) 1 August 1980 p. 24.
5   *Official Journal of the European Communities* No. C326/106 (31 December 1979)
6   *Op cit* para. 7.8.
7   FAO *Food Aid Bulletin* No. 2 (April 1980) Table 1.
8   Regulation (EEC) No. 1009/67.
9   House of Lords Select Committee on the European Communities: *EEC Sugar Policy* (London, HMSO, 19 March 1980), p. 18, para. 14.
10 *Ibid.* p. xii, para. 17.
11 House of Lords Select Committee on the European Communities, *EEC Sugar Policy: Minutes of Evidence*, Session 1979–80 (London, HMSO), p. 4, para. 7.
12 House of Lords Select Committee on the European Communities: *EEC Sugar Policy* (London, HMSO, 19 March 1980) p. XXV, para. 45 (ii).
13 Europe Information *Sugar, The European Community and the Lome' Convention* (19/79) Brussels p. 9.
14 Com (79) 130 final, 14 March 1979, p. 1.
15 Emphasis added.
16 See Mike Faber and Roland Brown 'Changing the Rules of the Game' *Third World Quarterly* Vol. 11 No 1 (London, January 1980) pp. 100–119.

2

EEC Industrial Policy and the Third World

E. Verreydt and J. Waelbroeck

The strong political pressures exerted by ailing domestic industries on the EEC for protection against imports have led to a stiffening of protection of some industries. The poor economic climate and the serious difficulties encountered by these industries have created a favourable climate for protection. This has to some extent been offset by the free trade bias of the EEC. After all, the Community was set up as a device for bringing about the free movement of goods, persons and capital, and it has on the whole tried not to deviate too much from this mandate. An alternative to protection (which we may call negative adjustment) would have been a vigorous policy of positive adjustment in manufacturing industry to cope with increases of imports. The Community however does not have the strong policy instruments required for such policies. It does not have the regional financial means. Two special funds had been set up initially: the European Social Fund and the ECSC reconversion and re-adaptation fund, set up under the Rome and ECSC Treaties respectively. In 1975, a European Regional Fund was created to provide resources for regional development, but it is a good deal smaller than initially envisaged. Recently, the Community started a new fund, the 'Ortoli Facility'. The European Investment Bank could also be useful in financing particular investments. Existing studies suggest, however, that these various funds are not very effective in promoting investment. The sums which they can distribute are not large. More importantly, it seems difficult to encourage potential users to make effective use of the system.

The treaty provisions which empower the EEC to prevent market distortions are a significant policy instrument at a time when the subsidies granted by governments are large. The EEC Directorate General for Competition monitors inter alia government aids and subsidies, with disputes being put before the Court of Justice. It is of course not possible to monitor all schemes (there are more than 1200 laws in force in the 9 member countries . . .) but the Commission can control the larger, more visible ones. This increases the transparency and smoothness of the EEC market, and limits domestic protection through subsidies and other devices; it is probable that this facilitates imports not only by EEC members, but also by third countries. Under the Rome Treaty, the Commission is responsible for regulating the foreign trade of the Community. Its autonomy in this field has however been gradually reduced as GATT negotiations have lowered (and made more uniform) tariff rates in different countries, and begun to bring about growing administrative uniformity in the system. In judging EEC policies, therefore, it is important to keep in mind the limited range of instruments available to the Commission. Most of the Community's budgetary resources are connected with and tied up by the Common Agricultural Policy. The main powers given to the Community by the Rome Treaty are control of foreign trade policy and a role of watchdog responsible for the regulation of competition. Thanks to the ECSC Treaty, the Community enjoys considerably greater power to regulate the steel and coal industries, but this does not extend to other types of energy. Thus the nuclear research organisation created by the Euratom treaty has through-out most of its life been paralysed by French obstruction. This example typifies the difficulties which hamstring the Community in taking initiatives in favour of industries which have a promising future. The treaties under which the Community was set up simply do not give it the power needed to undertake 'Japan Inc.' or French 'Contrat de Programme' type of industrial planning. Any attempt to set up such policies appears to stir up national jealousies which doom it to failure.

Adjustment in hard hit industries

Despite these difficulties, the Community has erected barriers to trade. The new protection measures introduced by the EEC have been motivated by severe problems in a few manufacturing sectors. Two of these – textiles and shoes – are low wage industries which do not require high labour skills and in which developing countries have a natural comparative advantage. The two others – steel and shipbuilding – are capital goods sectors which as such are naturally sensitive to business cycle downturns. Developing countries have a small share of world markets for the latter goods, but this situation may change, in particular for shipyards. It has often been remarked that the EEC has tended to be more active in nursing lame ducks than in promoting sectors which may become poles of future growth for the Community. Partly to answer this criticism, the Commission has sought to give visibility to its scheme of promoting the 'telematics' industry which is emerging as a result of the coming together of computer and telecommunication technologies. But it remains substantially true that the lame ducks predominate in Com-munity protection policies.

Textiles, clothing, shoes

The textiles and clothing industry has suffered from structural difficulties for a long time. It is a mature industry, in which the income elasticity of demand is not high while technical progress is swift. Entry into the industry is easy, making for a climate of keen competition. There is competition within the Common Market from low wage Italian producers who to a large extent evade taxes and social security obligations. Finally, the industry is probably the one which is most exposed to competition from developing countries. According to a widely held view, the textile and clothing industry in the EEC would crumble to the ground if it was exposed to open competition from developing countries. This view does not make allowance for the very great diversity within the industry. Large subsectors would indeed largely disappear; mostly those producing the 'highly sensitive goods' of the EEC Multifibre Agreement (MFA). But the fact that EEC exports and imports are in rough balance shows that there are subsectors which can meet competition from developing countries without any tariff protection. It should be remembered that effective tariffs on clothing are of the order of 20 %, so that domestic producers would still retain substantial protection even if the MFA quantitative controls were relaxed. Several branches of the industry are fairly capital intensive using the most up to date technologies. Specialisation is often an asset: German industrial textiles, and carpet making on the 'carpet freeway' in Flanders are strong and expanding subsectors. Adjustment in the textile industry is made difficult by its regional concentration. There is also a high percentage of female labour for which it is likely to be difficult to find alternative employment since unemployment rates for women substantially exceed rates for men. On the other hand, the industry requires few special skills, making adjustment easier, and it pays very low wages, which makes movement out of the industry easier to accept than in a high wage industry like steel.

Reference to the period when imports were more loosely controlled than today belies the claim that imports from developing countries are the main cause of unemployment. By an overwhelming margin, it has been technical progress which has caused the shrinkage of employment in the textiles and clothing sector. This progress will continue. Indeed, it is expected that the industry will be one of the first to be affected by the microchip revolution, opening the way to highly capital intensive ways of producing certain textile and clothing goods for which developing countries would normally not have a comparative advantage. It is not true, therefore, that the survival of the industry depends on the continuation of the present very stiff protection measures. It is more correct to state that if competition was more open, the EEC would not be able to maintain in existence 'a full range of textile production'. Levi's jeans and Arrow shirts, standard cotton cloth, etc. can be produced more cheaply in developing countries. Does this matter? Industry lobbyists are keen to raise up the spectre of an incomplete textile industry, but this spectre does not frighten trade economists.

The most vocal advocates of protection have been in Britain, where resistance to change has been greatest since the war. German producers, who have been the quietest, have been extremely effective in reorienting production by using outward processing to reduce labour costs, or by shifting to more specialised products. It is interesting that the German industry has been one of the few in the EEC which has registered a gain of output. This suggests that a willingness to adjust pays off in terms of growth. Adjustment is indeed inescapable. Trade unions cannot block the technological change which is around the corner, because there are too many EEC countries. Workers in the North will not be able to escape competition from Italy and the three Mediterranean entrants: Greece, Spain and Portugal. Large segments of the industry can be expected to migrate South over the next two decades, as has happened in the USA.

From a long term perspective, the main need is to have producers and trade unions understand that, as change is inevitable, they had best grasp the nettle and prepare to adjust. Textiles and clothing is a highly fragmented industry, which is almost impervious to schemes based on persuasion by planners. The best way to have the industry progress is to make it understand that the need to adjust will not be eliminated by protection and other interferences with market mechanisms. From this point of view the coming MFA III negotiations will be an important signal of the determination of governments to force producers to adjust – or of their yielding to the powerful political pressures which the industry is capable of exerting. The negotiations will also be an important signal for the developing countries. As the 'first sector of industrialisation', textiles and clothing have a vital role to play in the early stage of the export drive of new exporters of manufactured goods. What MFA II did was to freeze a geographic pattern of imports into the EEC by allocating the lion's share of textiles and clothing quotas to the early starters. Not surprisingly, other countries are feeling that the road is now closed, and are tempted to look for autarkic approaches to planning of future growth. The outcome of the MFA III negotiations will have an important bearing on whether the developing countries integrate their economies gradually into the world economy or whether most of them evolve into closed economies isolated from the world. Moreover, it may be asked whether it is in the interests of the Northern members of the Community to tighten protection further for textiles and clothing in order to save industries in their countries whose chances of long run survival seem poor even if protection is reinforced.

The synthetic fibres sector is undergoing a severe crisis in EEC countries, and has resorted to a cartel to deal with the situation. The EEC at one time envisaged giving its blessing to this cartel, then decided not to do so openly as this would hardly be compatible with its mandate under the Treaty of Rome. The cartel came into being anyway, and the

Commission is watching its actions with obviously ambivalent feelings.

The EEC shoe industry includes Italy, one of the lowest cost shoe producers in the world; and will in a few years include Spain, another competitive producer. Producers in the Northern EEC countries are not in such a strong position but realise that they cannot insulate themselves from competitive pressures. Given the fact that tariff rates for shoes are rather high, it does not appear that the industry's survival depends on the existence of permanent quantitative import controls. Yet, in the wake of the 1977 spate of textiles and clothing VER agreements, the European governments have moved to impose such agreements on the main shoe exporters in the world.

Steel

The steel industry, geared to the needs of the investment goods sector, has been hit by the global recession. The EEC steel industry in addition suffers from special structural problems. It consists in reality of two very different parts. The older and larger component was built up close to sources of coal and iron ore which have vanished, or are now more costly than imported materials. These factories, which were built at a time when the optimal scale of output was far smaller than today, have crowded plant which is not as conveniently laid out as factories built on greenfield sites. Productivity is in many instances held back by work practices to which trade unions have been clinging in spite of the evolution of technology. During the long postwar years of prosperity, the unions were well placed to resist technical changes which would have eliminated jobs. Opposition to rationalisation has continued in the recession, with less success. The newer component of the industry consists of a number of efficient large plants on the seacoast. These embody the latest technology, and process low cost imported materials. Production costs appear to be significantly lower than in the older inland plants. The EEC steel industry remains a large net exporter to the rest of the world. These exports have been hit, however, by keen competition from Japan's more recent, and hence more modern, steel industry. The inefficiency of the US steel industry has enabled European producers to seize part of its domestic market, but further gains have been blocked by the US trigger price/VER system. Sales to developing countries have been limited by the rapid growth of domestic production, and some of these countries (e.g. Korea, Brazil, India) have even begun to export steel.

Nonetheless, the European steel industry remains relatively competitive, particularly by comparison with the United States' industry. The recession for example, has led to sweeping price cuts, and losses which were so high that they wiped out the capital of the older Belgian mills in a couple of years, but even at these low prices the newer coastal mills were apparently able to make both ends meet. However, it would hardly be correct to describe the industry as a textbook case of perfect competition. A rapid concentration of ownership has been under way since the war, through nationalisation as well as through mergers. By now the industries in France, the UK, Italy and Belgium, which account for a very large share of output, are largely state-owned. Only the German and Dutch steel industries remain largely privately owned. Since the war steel has, of course, been the object of constant government attention, reflecting the peculiar concern of planners for the industry. This concern was manifested via lavish low interest credits and other aids to expansion and modernisation.

Thanks to the ECSC treaty, the Community has greater control over the steel (and coal) industries than over other sectors of the economy.In particular it can regulate price fixing, and control production and investment. The Davignon Plan used these powers to force through a sweeping restructuring of the industry: production controls coupled with control of both the quantities and price of imported steel have lifted prices above the very low levels which prevailed in 1977. For their part, producers have to cut excess workers, and to reduce excess capacity by closing down marginal plants. Whether the Davignon Plan will become permanent is uncertain at present. It could evolve into a second CAP, holding up domestic prices at a high and stable level and dumping surpluses on world markets. Such a development would not be in the Community's interest, however. Not only is steel one of its significant direct exports, but it is also the primary raw material of the metal fabricating industry, a very large exporter. It is important for the Community's competitiveness to keep domestic steel prices in line with world levels in the long run. This is not just an academic argument; steel users understand their need for reasonably priced raw materials, and will be willing to engage in countervailing lobbying if required. Germany is the largest exporter of metal products, and it is not surprising therefore, that the German representatives in the EEC have been insisting so strongly on a firm link between the renewal of the Davignon Plan and continuing progress in rationalising output. In practice, rationalisation has made reasonable progress. Governments and employers have not hesitated to confront trade unions on the issue of productivity, forcing through employment cuts in spite of major strikes in Germany, France and the UK. There appears to be a definite possibility that the Common Market steel industry will not follow the pattern which seems to be establishing itself in the US of gradual, permanent isolation from world markets. The main uncertainty lies in the EEC's ability to force through the cuts in production capacity which are required to re-establish the balance between supply and demand.

What are the interests of the developing countries in all this? For the present, they are being confronted by what is, in effect, a de facto OECD steel cartel, which regulates world prices and trade. As net importers, they lose by the price raising impact of the production restrictions imposed by the control. A few of them have also lost export sales because of the VER agreements which were forced on them. There is a fear in Europe that as steel production rises in the developing countries, they will take export markets away from the traditional producers. This may happen to some extent as a result of the energy crisis. Oil producing countries without a good outlet for their natural gas and with abundant capital may use these resources to produce steel, using the sponge iron process for the reduction of ore. There are success stories which suggest that this is feasible. Countries like India which have very favourable ore and coking coal resources may be tempted to imitate them, at a heavy price in scarce capital. It would indeed be to Europe's advantage to relocate some of its basic steel fabricating capacity – but to Australia rather than to the developing countries. On the whole, however, transport of ore and coking coal by bulk carriers is cheap enough to keep Europe's coastal plants competitive with factories elsewhere, and it is not likely that developing countries will make a decisive breakthrough in this market. What may take place instead is a fairly extensive relocation of the basic steel processes from the older inland European mills to countries with cheap natural gas, to Australia, but mostly to coastal plants. This would leave the inland mills to exploit their close contacts with users by specialising in the supply of rolled products and special steels.

Shipbuilding

The shipbuilding industry has been hit hard by the slowdown in the rate of growth of world trade. Activity was sustained in the early phase of the recession by running down order books, but this created a surplus of tonnage, especially for tankers, which then had to be absorbed. The adjustment has been painful, with the closing down of major yards and consequent unemployment. The industry is strongly concentrated geographically and has powerful trade unions. Not surprisingly, it has a long record of government interference. The long postwar decline of British shipbuilding was mainly due to the strength of Japanese competition, but also to competition from continental builders who benefitted directly or indirectly from subsidy schemes. The recession triggered an escalation of competing subsidy schemes, which on occasions have covered a surprisingly large proportion of a ship's price, in spite of the moderating influence of the EEC's regulation on aids to industry. The UK industry was nationalised; a logical consequence of heavy government support. In recent years, governments appear to have become more aware of the pointlessness of continuing heavy support of an industry which needs to adjust anyway. In fact, thanks to (or in spite of) governments' programmes, the Common Market shipbuilding industry has made substantial progress in reducing excess capacity and rationalising production.

At the world level, the size of the industry depends on the growth of world trade. Unless current trends change, therefore, it will be permanently smaller than in the 1960's and early 1970's. This is an area in which developing countries have potentially a comparative advantage. Building ships is not a capital intensive activity. The increased use of prefabricated elements has reduced the need for special skills. An increasing number of developing countries have built up efficient steel industries, which could produce the special plates needed for building ships. Finally, there is probably an advantage in being a later starter in a heavily unionised sector, where older producers are handicapped by strong trade union defence of obsolete work practices (this was an important asset for Japan in achieving its spectacular breakthrough as a shipbuilder after the war).

A number of developing countries – Korea, Brazil, India – and also socialist countries such as Poland and the USSR have built up efficient shipbuilding industries and are beginning to export ships, and they appear to be doing well in today's difficult market. They are fortunate in that this is an industry which is very difficult to protect. Its client – shipping – is a world market activity par excellence. There is little point in protecting domestic shipbuilders by tariffs, as this would make national shipping firms uneconomic, and national capital can always emigrate and escape government control by using a flag of convenience. It is for this reason that government aid has been extended via subsidies rather than via tariffs. Sometimes the subsidies have been highly indirect, such as the obligation to carry US aid on ships of the US flag, which has the effect of channelling to the national shipping and shipbuilding firms a part of the aid intended to help developing countries.

Unlike steel, the Community has no power to regulate production and investment in shipbuilding. Its ability to regulate the adjustment process depends on its power to regulate aids and subsidies, and to approve mergers, and will largely vanish when the current crisis ends. The Commission has nevertheless proposed a Community-wide scrap and build plan, which would reduce excess supply for shipping and bring about a resurgence of demand. The response of governments to this plan has not been enthusiastic, and it may not get off the ground. In any event, there is reason to believe that the worst of the crisis is over, and that the industry is entering a more stable period in which there will be less pressure on governments to think up special programmes of aid. The limited success of assistance granted in recent years, and the fact that in a number of instances it has led to clear excesses, involving politically unacceptable degrees of subsidy, makes it more difficult to sell to public opinion new schemes than it was a few years ago.

Will protectionism increase in 1981?

The recent protection record is certainly not rosy, but neither is it all black. Some restrictive measures have been taken, especially in 1977 and in the beginning of 1978. But given the persistent recession, there was temptation to do much more, and some credit must be given to officials in the EEC and in governments for containing the protectionist pressures to which they have been exposed. It is probably important that these interferences with trade mechanisms have taken the form of strengthening pre-existing mechanisms rather than introducing new techniques of protection or new legal triggering devices. One should note, however, the increasingly explicit way in which discriminatory import restrictions have been used, especially for textiles and for shoes, and the increasing openness with which EEC trade negotiators have asked that these practices be given legal standing under the GATT.

We will finally stick our necks out in saying that the trend of thinking in the EEC is once again (rather cautiously) moving towards a more liberal attitude to trade. The reason is that by and large the experiments in solving problems by protection, subsidies, and other devices, have not worked very well. There is a growing recognition that these manipulations are, at best, a costly way of postponing the inevitable. Recent election results suggest that this evolution in thinking has a broad base in public opinion. It is not our feeling that the EEC is headed toward imposing across-the-board restrictions on imports from developing countries. On the contrary, our expectations would be that these countries could negotiate some easing of existing restrictions if they pressed as hard as they have pressed for some of the more far fetched New International Economic Order proposals, and if they were willing in exchange to accept an easing of their own protectionism (a number of them are in fact eliminating unilateral trade restrictions which are often unreasonably high).

In 1981 MFA II will expire, and will certainly be replaced by a third Multifibre Agreement. The hue and cry by the industry has already begun, with the weakest textile and clothing industry, that of the UK, as the most vocal up to now. What the industry wants is the elimination of the flexibility in the import control scheme. From their point of view, the agreement with Mainland China is seen as a 'better mousetrap'; its details suggest that bureaucrats have thought of new, clever devices to control trade. It is probable that the EEC will press to have these devices extended to imports from other countries. On the other hand, the MFA scheme is formally set up under the GATT, and a certain measure of agreement by developing countries is necessary for renewal. The EEC does threaten to impose selective import controls unilaterally in violation of article 19 of the GATT if developing countries do not comply with its wishes, but it is clear that it is willing to go to some lengths to avoid this. Finally, developing countries, thanks to the expansion of their trade, are beginning to have some bargaining power, although this power is limited since the decisive phase of the import limitation process does not take place in a general GATT negotiation, but in an eyeball to eyeball confrontation between the EEC, with all its economic might, and each particular developing country.

The extreme demands of the textile and clothing industry will probably not be met. Nonetheless some tightening of import controls will probably be forced on developing countries as the EEC responds to domestic political pressure. These are serious and important questions for the developing world, and it is curious that they are not raised in any detail in the catalogue of demands which developing countries have asked to be discussed in the forthcoming Global Negotiations.

3

The Second Lomé Convention

Adrian Hewitt and Christopher Stevens

The choice of the Togolese capital of Lomé as the venue for signing the second Convention between the EEC and the ACP may turn out to be symbolic. The provisions of Lomé II resemble closely those of its predecessor, Lomé I. The main differences are to be found in the details, which in general have been improved, and in the morale of the two sides, which has worsened considerably. This chapter analyses the negotiating process; sets out the main provisions of Lomé II in the context of experience under Lomé I; and forecasts the likely impact of the new Convention.

Negotiating Lomé II

Lomé I was signed on February 1975 with a fanfare of self-congratulation. It grew from the twin roots of the pre-existing relation-ship of the Six with France's African colonies in the Treaty of Rome, subsequently modified after they became independent by the establish-ment of the Yaoundé Conventions, and out of the need to make provisions for Britain's former colonies when the Six expanded to Nine. Commonwealth ldcs were split into the 'associables' and the 'non-associables', and the former group, in Africa and scattered over the Caribbean and the Pacific (hence the acronym ACP) joined with the Yaoundé countries in the new Lomé Convention. The 'non-associables' were offered a range of different and non-contractual trade/aid régimes (all less favourable than Lomé) by the Nine described in Chapter 4. It is this discrimination in treatment between the associables and other members of the Group of 77 that underlies much of the criticism of the Lomé Conventions, and to which the final section of this chapter turns.

The first Lomé Convention was unique in some respects, but much of the euphoria greeting it was quite misplaced. It was a multilateral package of measures covering aid, trade, and industrial co-operation. This was something of an innovation. Moreover, it established a set of consultative fora, with the promise of a continuing, effective and productive dialogue between the two sides. And, of course, there were some tempting morsels in the small print: the Stabex scheme, and more favourable trade access to the Community's market for the ACP than for any of the other blocs with which the EEC trade. It also represented, at the time, the beginnings of a concerted policy at Community level towards the developing world.

But while Lomé I possessed valuable features and, putting aside the wider issue of those ldcs outside its charmed circle, represented a perfectly respectable deal for the ACP, it was in no sense a 'road to Damascus' conversion for either side. The continuity from Yaoundé II is as evident as the change. Writing of Lomé II, the former Director of the European Development Fund (EDF), Jacques Ferrandi, has argued 'Elle ressemblera, comme une soeur jumelle à l'actuelle Convention de Lomé, laquelle ressemblait, comme une grande soeur, à la Convention de Yaoundé'.[1]

It is a common tendency for institutions as well as for individuals to inflate their achievements, and usually no harm is done thereby. However, the Lomé II negotiations were made more difficult and more acrimonious than they need otherwise have been because both sides had

Table 3.1 *Who are the ACP?*

(a) Defined as 'least developed'

*Benin	*Ethiopia	*Mauritania	*Sudan
*Botswana	*Gambia	*Niger	*Swaziland
*Burundi	*Grenada	*Rwanda	*Tanzania
Cape Verde	*Guinea	St Lucia	*Togo
*Central African Republic	*Guinea-Bissau Kiribati	Sao Tome Principe Seychelles	*Tonga Tuvalu
*Chad	*Lesotho	*Sierra Leone	*Uganda
Comoros	*Malawi	Solomon Islands	*Upper Volta
Djibouti	*Mali	*Somalia	*Western Samoa
Dominica			

(b) Landlocked or island countries, not defined as 'least developed'

*Bahamas	*Jamaica	*Mauritius	*Trinidad & Tobago
*Barbados	*Madagascar	Papua-New Guinea	*Zambia
*Fiji			

(c) Others

*Cameroon	*Ghana	*Kenya	*Senegal
*Congo	*Guyana	*Liberia	Suriname
*Equatorial Guinea	*Ivory Coast	*Nigeria	*Zaire
*Gabon			

Notes: The EEC have agreed to consider treating Zaire as a landlocked country, although it quite clearly cannot be defined as such. Kiribati, Vanuatu and Zimbabwe have joined since Lomé II was signed.

* Original signatory of Lomé I.

been taken in by their own rhetoric. The ACP entered the negotiations with the stated aim of building upon Lomé I. A formal start was made to the negotiations at a ministerial conference in Brussels commencing 27 July 1978. The ACP negotiating posture was made clear by its spokesman, P. J. Patterson of Jamaica, in his opening address when he warned that 'all too often yesterday's innovation becomes today's orthodoxy and tomorrow's anachronism'. And he continued:

> To the ACP group therefore, the Lomé Convention always represented no more than a step, albeit a significant one, towards their goal. It is not its final achievement, though let me hasten to acknowledge, it represented an example to the rest of the developed world which unfortunately has not been followed.
> Today our sole purpose here is to seek to make with you, our partners, another significant step towards that urgently needed goal.[2]

From the outset, it was clear that this view of the negotiations differed fundamentally from that held by the EEC. H. D. Genscher, the then chairman of the EEC Council explained the Community's position in his welcoming address. 'We are prepared to continue and extend further the co-operation launched under the Lomé Convention', he said, but then continued 'The Convention has proved itself in practice. The negotiations *will therefore not deal* with sweeping changes or renovations, but with adjustments and improvements.'[3]

The words 'will therefore not deal' have been emphasised because they encapsulate the tone of the Community negotiating style, at least until Easter 1979: a blunt take-it-or-leave-it approach which made few attempts to slip a velvet glove over the iron hand. Four factors contributed to the sour atmosphere in which the negotiations were concluded. First and most fundamentally, the Nine were unwilling to make any major new concessions. In general, their perceptions of the continuing world recession urged retrenchment in dealings with the South rather than the kind of imaginative, large-scale transfers and concessions that were being widely recommended[4] to facilitate trade expansion, break the protectionist spiral and unleash the dynamic forces of the market. Second, the EEC has an in-built institutional bias that favours the creation of impasse. The procedure is for the Commission to propose to the Council a set of negotiating positions, on the basis of which the Council issues the Commission with a 'mandate' for negotiation that provides only limited leeway for manoeuvre. Hence the Commission has to refer back to the Council whenever the negotiations reach a stalemate and a new initiative is required. Furthermore, members of the Council need an occasion to refer back to their national capitals before such decisions can be taken.

Because of the Nine's reluctance to make concessions, the Commission's negotiating mandate for Lomé II was much more tightly drawn than had been its Lomé I mandate. Moreover, it has been argued that the Commission omitted to take advantage of what little flexibility its mandate bestowed. Hence the third factor contributing to the bad feeling was the rigid and, according to some, high-handed attitude of EEC negotiators. Whereas Commissioner Claude Cheysson, the political head of DG VIII (the Directorate-General for Development), had played a leading role in formulating Lomé I, the negotiations for its successor were left largely in the hands of Commission officials. Cheysson only became closely involved after the talks had reached an impasse at Easter 1979. By which time, it was too late for him to avoid being regarded by the ACP as a 'fire brigade' and, moreover, one that was operating largely at the behest of President Giscard d'Estaing to ensure that the negotiations were sewn up before the end of France's term as president of the Council of Ministers; a task in which he only just failed.

Finally, the ACP played their hand badly. At the early negotiating sessions they appeared to be in disarray. Apparently they were advised by a senior Third World figure not to accept automatically the EEC's timetable for the talks, and not to assume that the Community had nothing at stake in the negotiations. At the early sessions, the ACP appeared not to have heeded either piece of advice. The result was that the Community's confidence in the strength of its position turned into over-confidence. The denoument came in May 1979 when, to the demonstrable surprise of the Community, the ACP rejected its aid offer. On May 24 ministers from both sides came together for what was billed as the final round of talks. But two days later the discussions were adjourned and no date was set for their resumption. Observers claim that ACP emotions ran high, and that the rejection of the aid offer was a symbol of their dissatisfaction on a much wider range of issues, not least the way in which the various ministerial and ambassadorial meetings had been conducted, and the way in which ACP demands were flatly rejected.

Clashes over renewal versus renegotiation, over negotiating style and over the size of the Community's aid pledge for the next five years stole the headlines but several other important issues preoccupied the negotiators. The EEC sought policy changes in four main areas. First, improved contractual arrangements to protect (and therefore encourage) European investment (particularly that of mining companies) in ACP countries. Second, the establishment of an obligatory consultative mechanism between ACP governments and EEC producers/consumers as a means of avoiding any impending import 'threat' to the EEC from the manufactured or processed agricultural exports of the ACP. Third, the insertion of a 'social clause', drawn from relevant ILO conventions, into Lomé II; and, fourth, the addition of a control mechanism linking ACP governments' receipt of aid to the observation of human rights in individual ACP countries. In the course of the negotiations the social and human rights clauses were simply dropped as impractical, partly for reasons of internal disputes between the EEC member states. The third part of this chapter examines the EEC's progress on its other two demands.

For their part, the ACP sought four general reforms. First, completely free trade access to the Community for all ACP products (i.e. entry free of tariffs, levies and quantitative limits) together with less restrictive rules of origin requirements. Second, abolition of the general safeguard clause governing ACP imports to the EEC. Third, extension of Stabex to all products, ideally based on exports to all destinations (including extra-EEC markets) and indexation of Stabex transfers. Finally, the establishment of special funds earmarking aid for industrial investment, for commercial promotion, for regional projects affecting more than one ACP country, and a separate aid fund at the disposal of the least developed, island and landlocked countries. In addition, the ACP presented proposals of interest to individual states – levy-free access for Botswana's beef, for Senegalese tomatoes and softer aid/Stabex terms for Zaire on the grounds that it is *nearly* landlocked. The Community found it easier to respond to these relatively minor particularist proposals than to the ACP's four general demands, on none of which were any significant concessions made: The absence of real dialogue on these issues was another factor leading the ACP to focus all their frustration on the question of the aid package.

The aid package, offered by the EEC as a 'non negotiable' first and final word on the subject and rejected by the ACP in May 1979, was Eua 5,100 million. Following its rejection, Commissioner Cheysson began to play a more active role, and partly because of his efforts the two sides returned to the negotiating table on 25 June 1979. Another factor contributing to the reduction of the conflict was that the aid package appeared to have been boosted by Eua 507 million. Although this 'increase' was as much cosmetic as real (see below) it was enough to save face for both sides. Even so, the new Convention was not in the bag. After two days the talks broke up in confusion. The EEC had been so confident of success that the then chairman of the Council of Ministers, French Foreign Minister, Jean François-Poncet, who left the meeting before it ended, gave a confident press conference at which he declared the negotiations to have been concluded successfully, only to be embarrassed a few hours later when the ACP spokesman, Senegalese Finance Minister, Ousmane Seck, firmly stated that the two sides had not reached agreement. From July to October, therefore, the talks were in a curious limbo. The EEC officially maintained that they had been concluded; the ACP stated that this was not so. Throughout the four months, discussions continued at an official level, and even delayed the signing ceremony by two hours. Nevertheless, despite their revolt from May onwards, in the end the ACP signed on the dotted line on 31 October 1979 and agreed to terms that on essential points were very similar to those initially offered by the EEC. The Lomé II Convention enters into force when two thirds of the ACP (i.e. at least forty states) and all the EEC governments ratify it. In the meantime, transitional arrangements embodied in Community legislation enable the trade provisions granted under Lomé I to continue, and the aid allocation from the fourth EDF (Lomé I) gives rise to spending decisions although the fifth EDF cannot yet be constituted.

Lomé I in practice

The negotiations for Lomé II were hampered because they began when only very preliminary indications of the impact of Lomé I were available. The first Lomé Convention contained the provision that negotiations on its successor should commence eighteen months before it expired. Bearing in mind that the signatories had to establish their negotiating position before this deadline, and that the effective duration of the aid provisions of Lomé I was only four years, this meant that crucial decisions had to be taken before the Convention had run more than half its course, and before any very useful trade and aid data were available. Since then enough material has become available to gauge some of the effects of the convention.

Trade

The Lomé trade régime is superficially very liberal. The ACP benefit from easier access to the Community market than is offered to any other ldc group. The EEC is fond of pointing out that 99.5 % of ACP exports enter the Community duty free. However, this figure says more about the nature of current ACP exports than it does about the value of the Lomé concessions. It is static and ignores the dynamic context of changes the ACP desire in the structure of their trade. The main influences constraining the EEC's trade liberalism are the common agricultural policy (CAP) and, to a small but increasing extent in the Lomé context, the pressures from declining European industries, notably textiles and clothing. In consequence, the Lomé trade régime is liberal in four main areas. First in cases where the commodities in question would enter the EEC market duty free in any case. Because the ACP are primarily exporters of raw materials (see Table 3.2), the proportion of goods falling into this category is very high – in the region of 75 %. Over one-quarter of ACP exports to the EEC are accounted for by petroleum, (mostly from the ACP's two OPEC members, Nigeria and Gabon) which is not an import that the Community would normally want to restrict with or without a Lomé Convention! The second area of Lome trade liberalism concerns products that do not have unrestricted access, but which would be imported in the normal course of events (because an EEC demand exists which cannot be satisfied locally) but which need not be obtained from the ACP. Examples are cocoa and bananas for which ACP exporters have a tariff preference over Latin American producers.[5] In such cases the 'cost' of the Lomé privilege is borne not by the EEC but by third party exporters.

The third area is where the ACP are ill-placed to take advantage of the benefits on offer. This particularly concerns industrial products which are accorded free access under the Convention. The trouble is that the ACP's capacity to export industrial products is very limited. There are few

Table 3.2 *Commodity Composition of ACP Exports to EEC (1977)*

Product	% by value	Cumulative %
Oil	28.1	28.1
Coffee	16.1	44.2
Cocoa	10.2	54.4
Copper	7.6	62.0
Timber	5.0	67.0
Sugar	3.1	70.1
Iron Ore	3.0	73.1
Groundnuts	2.8	75.9
Aluminium	2.2	78.1
Cotton (excl. fabrics)	1.9	80.0

Source: Analysis of trade between the European Community and the ACP States.
Series: Trade Flows
(Eurostat, Luxembourg 1979) p. 5.4.

obvious common factors linking the 60 countries scattered over three continents, and setting them apart from other ldcs. But one such link is the lower than average share of manufactures in their exports; since they are all relatively small economies – with the exception of Nigeria – the absolute volume of their manufactured exports is also very small. The World Bank has published figures on the manufactured exports of the larger ldcs in 1976. Of the 32 ldcs which it classifies as low income countries, 11 are ACP. In both categories, the difference in the average value of manufactured exports between the ACP and non-ACP is striking. In the low income group, the 1976 average for the ACP is $30 million against $365 million for the non-ACP. And even if the larger economies of India, Pakistan and Bangladesh are excluded from the analysis the non-ACP average is still $40 million. In the middle income group the disparity is even greater: $87 million for the ACP against $1195 million for the others.[6] Not surprisingly, therefore, manufactures do not figure prominently in ACP exports to the EEC despite the tariff concessions. This need not necessarily be considered a fault in the Convention, particularly if the trade concessions had the effect of encouraging the development of processing and manufacturing industries in the ACP. However, the signs are that in cases where an ACP is able to take advantage of its theoretical rights, it runs the risk of administrative action to discourage it. Although it is a contractual agreement the Convention is substantially subject to interpretation by the EEC. Clothes and cotton textiles form a high proportion of the small amount of ACP manufactured exports. The quantities involved are not large. In 1977 clothes accounted for 0.37% by value of total EEC imports from the ACP, while the share of cotton textiles was 0.25%. But the rate of growth from this very low base has been quite rapid. Between 1975 and 1977 the volume of clothing exports rose by 93 %, while for cotton textiles the increase was 33 %.[7] As a result, the Community has leaned on Ivory Coast to discourage it from developing an export capacity. The experience of Mauritius has been even more severe: exports have been held up in customs sheds until the suppliers agreed to 'voluntary' export restraints. In mid-1980 there were reports that the EEC was planning to supercede this system of pressure by one of formal quotas for ACP clothing and textile exports.[8]

The fourth area is the most significant. Some real access concessions are granted to the ACP which might not have been available in the absence of the Convention, and which are not necessarily obtained at the expense of other ldcs. These cover some of the products that fall within the purview of the Common Agricultural Policy (CAP). This is a relatively small area – accounting for 9 % of ACP exports to the Community – but it is of some importance for particular countries. Examples are Botswana (beef) and the Caribbean (sugar).[9] Not surprisingly, the trade concessions are complex and closely tailored to safeguard European farming interests.

The proof of any trade package is in its impact on trade flows. Speaking at the signing ceremony for the first Lomé Convention, the then President of the European Commission, Francois-Xavier Ortoli, claimed that 'although financial aid remains necessary, and even fundamental, for a certain number of particularly poor countries, it cannot remain the only method of development co-operation. That is why we wanted to open the European market to products from the ACP states and give them access to our know-how and technology in a framework of intensive industrial co-operation.'[10] Claims that the EEC has thrown open its market can be tested against events. By the same token claims made by observers of a quite different persuasion that Lomé is a device to tie parts of the Third World more tightly to Europe in a relationship of dependency can be compared with actual performance.

It must be stated at the outset that although some data are now available for trade flows under Lomé I, it is still very early to begin making definitive judgments. All conclusions on the impact of Lomé on trade must be tentative. This said, it is difficult to discern from the data available so far any particular impact of Lomé I on trade flows either for good or for ill. Table 3.3 shows total flows for the years 1972–77. It indicates that the EEC's imports from the ACP have risen faster than average, but there is no significant difference between the pre- and post-Lomé periods for the ACP's performance relative to total imports or to imports from all ldcs. When it comes to EEC exports, however, there is a marked difference between the years before Lomé was signed and the period since. Between 1972 and 1974, EEC exports to the ACP grew more slowly than total exports, or exports to all ldcs. But between 1975 and 1977 this relationship was reversed, with the ACP market growing faster. Much of this growth can be attributed to increased EEC exports to ACP

Table 3.3 *EEC – ACP Trade: total flows 1972–77*

(Eua mn)	1972	1973	1974	1975	1976	1977	%change 1974/1972	%change 1977/1975
EEC Imports								
Total[a] of which:	65 573	84 306	130 802	125 451	159 590	171 230	100	37
industrialised countries	35 942	45 757	59 776	60 326	75 818	82 066	66	36
all developing countries	24 451	31 927	61 379	54 976	70 021	75 137	151	37
ACP (53)	4 890	6 171	10 500	8 711	10 472	12 461	115	43
state trading countries	5 032	6 484	8 883	9 237	12 362	13 254	77	43
EEC Exports								
Total[a] of which:	65 754	80 673	114 224	121 212	141 300	164 140	73	35
industrialised countries	40 844	49 785	66 531	62 505	74 131	85 596	63	37
all developing countries	19 045	22 948	35 213	44 068	50 951	61 780	85	40
ACP (53)	4 036	4 462	6 122	8 118	9 883	12 504	52	54
state trading countries	5 215	7 212	10 929	13 014	14 238	14 530	110	12

a = Total extra-EEC trade

Source: Analysis of Trade Between the European Community and the ACP states. Series: Trade Flows (Eurostat, Luxembourg 1979) p. 2.3.

Table 3.4 *Share of developing countries in EEC trade (%)*

	IMPORTS			EXPORTS		
	1972	*1973-76*	*1977*	*1972*	*1973–76*	*1977*
Total	100.0	100.0	100.0	100.0	100.0	100.0
Developing countries						
of which:	37.3	43.6	43.8	29.0	33.5	37.6
Ldc excl. OPEC	19.5	18.0	19.1	21.3	20.7	19.5
OPEC	17.8	25.6	24.7	7.7	12.8	18.1
ACP (53)	7.4	7.2	7.3	6.1	6.3	7.6
ACP excl. OPEC	5.1	4.6	5.0	4.9	4.4	4.5

Source: Analysis of Trade Between the European Community and the ACP States Series:
Trade Flows
  (Eurostat, Luxembourg 1979) p. 2.5.

oil producers. Table 3.4 shows that the proportion of EEC exports going
to the ACP (excluding OPEC members) actually fell between 1972 and
1977. It fell, moreover, by virtually the same proportion as did EEC
exports to all ldcs (excluding OPEC). And Table 3.4 also shows that
despite the higher than average increase in EEC imports originating in the
ACP, the rise was not sufficiently large to make any appreciable difference
in the ACP's share of total EEC imports.

Aid

Only part of the official aid (oda) given by the Nine to the ACP is
channelled through the EEC, and not all the finance provided under the
Lomé Convention is oda.[11] The proportion of national aid budgets
channelled through Community institutions (whether to the ACP or
other ldcs) varies widely between the Nine. In 1977, 45 % of Italy's oda,
but only 5.4 % of Denmark's, went through the EEC. For the four largest
donors, the proportions in 1977 were: France, 7.9 %, Germany, 16 %,
Britain, 10.5 % and Holland, 7.4 %.

The main questions to ask of Lomé with respect to aid are: first, has
Lomé increased the amount of aid spent either on the ACP or on ldcs as a
whole; and second, is aid disbursed through the EEC more or less effective
than aid disbursed bilaterally or through alternative multi-lateral institutions such as the World Bank? Some might wish to add a third question:
does it facilitate Community building in the EEC? Valid though this
approach may be, it is not one that is of any particular value to ldcs or to
the cause of development. The first question can only be answered after a
detailed analysis of donor disbursement performance. The creation of the
European Development Fund back in 1958, and its subsequent replenish-
ment did not perceptibly boost the overall aid 'effort' of any EEC member

state; displacement probably outweighed attraction. But the issue is not limited to the Lomé context. The proliferation of agencies, windows and facilities over the past two decades bears witness to a belief among many ldc governments that an increase in the number of aid agencies adds to the volume of aid. The standard response in the dcs has tended to be a denial of any such relationship, on the grounds that there exists a fixed aid cake. On the other hand, it is clear that, at the margin, the ACP countries, as opposed to the rest of the developing world, receive more aid thanks to the Lomé Convention than they would without it.

An evaluation of Lomé aid hinges largely upon its comparative effectiveness. This is also a difficult area, both because the comparison is with a range of donors with different performance standards, and because of the normative nature of the concept of 'aid effectiveness'. However, one fairly uncontroversial facet of effectiveness is speed of implementation, and on this count at least the EEC's performance under Lomé I has not been good. The EEC spends its oda in two main ways: conventional project aid, and the trade/aid hybrid of Stabex. The money is technically held in a European Development Fund (EDF), of which there have now been four, with a fifth agreed for the duration of Lomé II. EDF I was created under the Treaty of Rome, EDFs II and III under the Yaoundé Conventions, while EDF IV was coterminous with Lomé I. The distribution of *commitments* under EDF IV up to mid-1979 is shown in Table 3.5. The EEC likes to claim that the projects on which it spend its money are selected by the recipient country. To an extent this is probably true, but so it is for other donors. It is hard to discern any justification in the procedures and practice of the Community for the claim that the balance of power and choice between donor and recipient is significantly different from that which pertains with other donors. In fact article 108(5) of Lomé II states clearly 'The Community shall be responsible for preparing and taking financial decisions on projects and programmes.'

Table 3.5 *How Lomé I's EDF is being used*

Commitments as at mid-1979 by sector	Eua m	%
Production (agriculture and industry)	729	38
Transport infrastructure	383	20
Social services	304	16
Trade promotion	29	1
Disaster relief	98	5
Stabex	270	14
Administrative costs	106	6
Total committed	1919	100
Total available	3076	

Whoever selects the projects, the result so far has been to emphasise schemes involving a heavy input of infrastructure. A detailed study of EEC aid to Cameroon[12] for example, reveals that over the 18 years from 1958 when EDF aid first began to 1975, some 53 % of EEC aid spending was on transport infrastructure, followed at a long distance by education (mostly school buildings) with 15 %, rural agricultural production (13 %) and health (again mainly buildings) with 6 %. The period to which these figures refer is one which has seen a profound shift in thinking of many aid donors about the most effective ways of encouraging development. Table 3.5 suggests that the EEC's current practice is not as concentrated on infrastructure as the Cameroon example would suggest, but it also makes clear that infrastructure remains a high priority. The EEC appears to have changed its approach more slowly than some other major donors. The Cameroon study concludes that 'judged against the current criteria for aid effectiveness – sustained economic development, increases in local administrative competence, and improvement in the lot of the poor – the EDF's aid allocation mechanism seems to have missed the mark, predominantly because it failed to adapt to new circumstances and new development priorities'.[13]

To be honest, no one *knows* the most effective forms of aid spending. Africa undoubtedly still needs plenty of new transport infrastructure, and the EEC still possesses the machinery to supply it. Those involved with aid policy and analysis are groping their way towards what appear to be more effective avenues. But there are few absolutes and many relatives to guide them. It would be wrong, therefore, to condemn EEC aid simply on the grounds that it does not conform to current fashions. On many of the larger projects, EEC aid is simply one input lying cheek by jowl with, for instance, French or World Bank finance. On the other hand, if the use of EEC aid is to be compared to that of other donors it must be admitted that there is precious little evidence that it is more effective, and that what evidence does exist suggests that it may be less effective than some of the alternative channels for the aid provided by the Nine.

We are on much safer ground when the focus for analysis is shifted from use to speed of implementation. Fast spending is not the EDF's strong point. In reply to a written question in the European Parliament the Commission supplied figures on commitments and disbursements from EDF IV up to 30 September 1979 which are summarised in Table 3.6; fuller details on commitments and disbursements are given in the Statistical Appendix. Table 3.6 shows that of a total fund of Eua 3076m, only 64 % had been committed and 27 % disbursed by September 1979, which was just 6 months before Lomé I expired. And it must be borne in mind that these rates include expenditure on Stabex and the administrative costs of the EEC's quasi diplomatic delegations in the ACP, both of which are relatively fast spenders. The money disbursed through Stabex can be partially separated. In the period up to June 1979, eight states received 75 % of Stabex transfers (see below for details). Seven of these fall into the ex-British, ex-French categories of Table 3.6. If their Stabex receipts are deducted, the disbursement/commitment rate becomes 44% for the former French colonies and 31% for the former British colonies. Commitments tend moreover to be much higher (on a per capita basis) for the ex-French colonies than for the others: the EEC's treatment of

Table 3.6   *Commitments and Disbursements from EDF IV as at 30 September 1979*

Recipients	(Eua thousands)		
	Commitments	*Disbursements*	*Disbursements as a % of Commitments*
Former French colonies[a]	807 145	446 155	55
of which:			
Senegal	113 211	87 136	77
Niger	91 506	60 830	67
Mali	72 832	30 986	43
Guinea	56 423	10 749	19
Ivory Coast	56 148	26 895	48
Former British colonies[b]	652 712	216 521	33
of which:			
Tanzania	95 920	36 707	38
Kenya	79 931	25 354	32
Malawi	58 350	16 211	28
Zambia	54 219	21 150	39
Sudan	52 444	16 511	29
Former Belgian colonies[c]	208 331	64 073	31
of which:			
Zaire	96 970	23 502	24
Rwanda	67 932	25 873	38
Others[d]	149 070	50 958	34
of which:			
Ethiopia	74 869	26 077	35
Guinea-Bissau	26 074	11 620	45
Regional Projects	150 448	50 269	33
Total	1 967 706	827 976	42

Notes:

a – Benin, Cameroun, Central African Republic, Chad, Comoros, Congo, Djibouti, Gabon, Guinea, Ivory Coast, Madagascar, Mali, Mauritania, Niger, Senegal, Togo, Upper Volta.

b – Bahamas, Barbados, Botswana, Dominica, Fiji, Gambia, Ghana, Grenada, Guyana, Jamaica, Kenya, Lesotho, Malawi, Mauritius, Nigeria, Solomon Islands, Seychelles, Sierra Leone, Somalia, Sudan, Swaziland, Tanzania, Tonga, Trinidad, Tuvalu, Uganda, Zambia.

c – Burundi, Rwanda, Zaire.

d – Cape Verde, Ethiopia, Guinea-Bissau, Equatorial Guinea, Liberia, Papua New Guinea, Western Samoa, São Tomé, Surinam.

Source: Marchés Tropicaux (Paris) 11 January 1980, p. 69.

Rwanda is a favourable exception. If the full amount of Stabex disbursed at June 1979 (Eua 270m) is deducted from total commitments and disbursements, and the balance is expressed as a proportion of the EDF minus the Stabex element, the overall rates for commitments and disbursements are 63 % and 21 % respectively. In other words, almost four-fifths of the aid available to finance development projects remained to be spent although the Convention had almost run its course.

Is EEC aid spending biased in favour of France's favourites in general, and the former French colonies in particular? It has been alleged that this is the case, and it is certainly true that the ex-French colonies have been more successful at speeding up the Community's lumbering disbursement mechanism. But this is hardly surprising since they have accumulated experience of Community procedures and protocol under the Yaoundé conventions. Indeed, given this longer experience, the difference between the non-Stabex disbursement rate for the ex-French and ex-British colonies may be regarded as surprisingly small. However, if the focus is shifted to the actual amounts committed and disbursed the difference between the experience of these two groups of countries is much more marked. Table 3.7 sets out the comparison. Payments under the Stabex scheme have been removed from commitment and disbursement figures in Table 3.7, and for the per capita calculations the population of Nigeria has been removed since the Nigerian government took a conscious decision not to draw on EDF IV. It is quite clear from Table 3.7 that the ex-French colonies have done very much better than the ex-British colonies. The reasons for this disparity are less clear-cut than its existence. The francophone states (including the former Belgian colonies) clearly have more experience at working the EEC system, but while this may explain their much higher disbursement levels, it can hardly be a full explanation for the discrepancy in commitment levels. A similar bias appears in the award of EDF financed contracts. In the period up to the end of 1978, UK firms won only 9 % of EDF contracts against a UK

Table 3.7   *Aid per capita and per country: a comparison of francophone and anglophone states (EUA)*

Recipients	Aid per country		Aid per head	
	Commitments	Disbursements	Commitments	Disbursements
Former French colonies	40 340	17 778	10	5
Former British colonies[a]	24 039	7 382	6	2
Former Belgian colonies	69 444	21 358	6	2

Notes:
a – Excluding Nigeria.
b – Stabex payments to the major recipients have been deducted from commitments and disbursements. Ex-French colonies-Senegal, Mauritania, Niger, Benin, Ivory Coast, Gabon. Ex-British colony-Tanzania.
c – Population data from *World Bank Atlas*, 1979.

Table 3.8 *Breakdown of EDF IV funded contracts according to nationality of successful firms*

	% share of:				
Country	Works Contracts	Supply Contracts	Technical Cooperation Contracts	All Contracts	Contribution to EDF IV
Germany	14.6	31.95	25.08	20.37	25.95
Belgium	12.73	3.70	12.62	11.13	6.25
France	46.50	32.04	17.85	36.45	25.95
Italy	18.71	7.71	13.96	15.55	12.00
Luxembourg	–	–	2.73	0.72	0.20
Netherlands	3.51	3.31	10.55	5.33	7.95
Denmark	–	0.07	3.62	0.96	2.40
United Kingdom	3.95	21.22	11.98	9.07	18.70
Ireland	–	–	1.61	0.42	0.60

Notes: Data on award of contracts as at 31 December 1978 and excluding 'ACP' and 'Third Country' items. Breakdown of works and technical cooperation contracts is by nationality of contractor and of supply contracts is by origin of goods.

Sources: Supplement to the Official Journal of the European Communities (Luxembourg) S 88 Vol. 22, 10 May 1979 p. 3.
The Courier (Brussels) No. 31, March 1975, p. 33.

contribution to the Fund of 19%. By contrast, French firms won 37% of contracts as against a French contribution to the Fund of 26% (see Table 8), Indeed, there appears to be a clear division of the Nine into those that pay more into the EDF than they get out in terms of contracts (UK, Ireland, Denmark, Netherlands and Germany) and those for which the reverse is true (France, Belgium, Italy and Luxembourg). The Statistical Appendix gives a similar breakdown of contracts up to 31 December 1979 (including those awarded to non-EEC firms). It reveals that there has been some closing of the gap, but the division remains between France, Belgium, Italy and Luxembourg, and the rest. As with the country distribution of aid, the reasons for this discrepancy are less clearcut than its existence. A very plausible case has been made that the UK's low share of contracts derives from a low degree of interest among contractors who have been too preoccupied with rich pickings in the Middle East and elsewhere.

What does all this mean for ldcs? Is it important that the francophone ACP receive more than the anglophone ACP, provided that the funds are applied to worthwhile projects, and given that the EDF is only one channel for European aid funds? And does it matter to them one whit that some of the Nine are better at winning EDF contracts than others? The answer to the first question is that the distribution of aid between francophone and anglophone is suggestive of a lack of *development* (as opposed to *political*) focus in the EEC's allocation criteria. The EEC has no operationally effective, formalised criteria for distributing the total aid cake among the ACP. The criteria that actually govern the cake-slicing can only be judged from practice. And practice suggests that past colonial ties rather than, say, 'more aid to the poorest' is the most important criterion. As to the second question on contracts, the ACP have a direct interest to the extent that the discrepancies indicate an imperfect market for tenders which could lead to higher contract prices. However, perhaps more important is the prospect of increasing pressure inside the Nine to 'correct the anomalies'. The low UK share of contracts has been receiving increasing attention in Britain. A campaign to win a 'fair' share is a logical extension of the recent British government diplomatic offensive on the EEC budget, and of its stated policy that aid should be the handmaiden of foreign and commercial policy. The prospect is raised, therefore, of the Nine squabbling among themselves to ensure a 'fair share-out' of EDF funds rather than ensuring that the EDF is developmentally effective. In this event, the ACP would do far better to concentrate on the 'local costs' aspect of the EDF. Here the EEC's aid programme is considerably more liberal than that of most other donors. The ACP governments could, by influencing the design of projects at an earlier stage, ensure that their own contractors and suppliers could appropriate a greater share of EDF aid (they currently achieve 30% of the total) and thereby generate more production and employment at home.

One of the major innovations of Lomé I was the Stabex scheme, an aid-trade hybrid which provides partial compensation to exporters of a limited range of commodities when their prices fall. Like the IMF's much larger compensatory financing facility the stated goal of Stabex is to reduce export earnings instability, but unlike the IMF scheme it is related to the performance of individual products rather than to a country's export earnings as a whole. There are two reasons for this: first, the cost of a full-blooded export earnings scheme would be much greater; and second, the EEC's original idea had been to channel payments under Stabex to the producers of the affected commodities, but this linking ran into ACP opposition and was dropped during the Lomé I negotiations. Stabex is financed from the EDF. Disbursement is governed by a complex set of triggers and thresholds but, in theory at least, is automatic provided that these requirements are met. In practice, the Commission has some discretion in making an award, although this appears to have been exercised more to allow payments to states that did not fully satisfy the criteria rather than the other way around, eg Gabon's application for a Stabex transfer to compensate for a decline in timber exports in 1975 was initially rejected, but then approved in the full flush of the Lomé II negotiations, in June 1979. The scheme as approved during the Lomé I negotiations covered 12 commodities; this was extended to 19 in 1977.[14] The terms on which transfers are made vary: the 'least developed' ACP are not required to repay, and the trigger thresholds are lower for the least developed, landlocked and island states.

The mechanics of the scheme under Lomé I was as follows. For an individual commodity of a given ACP country to be covered it must account for 7.5% of all that country's merchandise export earnings (5% in the special case of sisal or 2.5% for the least developed, landlocked or island ACP states – over half of the total number). Further, there is a minimum level of earnings shortfall below which the Stabex payment will not be made. This is fixed at 7.5% for the larger ACP states with a coastline, and 2.5% for the others. Payments are only made to compensate for earnings shortfalls on supplies to the EEC, except for a dozen of the poorest ACP countries, for whom exports to all destinations count. Payments are made to governments, whose only obligation is to inform the EEC Commission of how the money has been used and, in the case of the richer countries, to repay the principal if and when their earnings in current prices from the commodity in question rise above the average of the previous four years. The country groupings, important for concessional treatment, are odd: Equatorial Guinea is classed as an island, and Togo (according to the World Bank a middle-income country) for EEC purposes benefits from the terms offered to the least developed. Because payments are made for individual commodity shortfalls, a state can receive Stabex compensation on one or several of the eligible products while the rest of its exports are booming and while its balance of payments may be enjoying a healthy surplus. And because the product coverage is limited, countries which export the 'wrong' goods may suffer severe earnings shortfalls yet be ineligible for any Stabex payment. Thus Ivory Coast was compensated for a shortfall in wood exports in 1975 even though its other main exports – cocoa and coffee – were booming, yet Zambia has received no payments despite the slump in the copper market because none of its exports are covered by the scheme. As a result of the limited coverage, and of the tendency that not all commodities are in a trough at the same time, Stabex payments have been concentrated on a small group of countries (see Statistical Appendix).

Despite these idiosyncracies the Stabex scheme is extremely popular among the ACP. Even those states that gain little or nothing from it have pressed not for its abolition but for its extension so that they, too, can benefit. The attractions of Stabex are obvious. Unlike the rest of the EDF it is a fast spender. Up to mid-1980 Stabex had made 107 transfers to 39 countries for 23 products to the value of Eua 387 million. Moreover, the transfers are effectively free foreign exchange for the recipients, allowing them the maximum flexibility in their use. And for the poorest countries the money is a grant. This cheapness is one reason why Stabex is much preferred by the ACP to the IMF's compensatory financing facility. The other is that the EEC does not poke around the dusty corners of the recipient's economic policy and recommend painful adjustments.

The innovations of Lomé II

In keeping with the opening position of the EEC that the negotiations were to deal only with 'adjustments and improvements', Lomé II is somewhat short on innovations. On trade issues, there have been some minor adjustments which should benefit a number of ACP countries. The only major change on the aid front has been that, despite the higher figures contained in the text, the amount on offer in real terms per capita has been cut by 21 % in comparison with the pledges of Lomé I. The most interesting changes come in the field of industrial co-operation. Even here the substance of what was agreed is more modest than it appears at first sight, but since the industrial co-operation provisions of Lomé I produced virtually no tangible results, the way under Lomé II can only be upwards.

Trade: a little more of the same

There may well have been little scope for major improvements to the existing Lomé trade régime. The ACP are already accorded duty free access to the European market for 75 % of their exports and in theory, if not in practice, for all their industrial exports. Moreover, a five-year Convention gives better access guarantees than preferences accorded to non-ACP states on an annual basis under GSP. (The relationship of Lomé to the EEC's other preferential trade accords is examined in Chapter 4.) The main product-area for valuable improvements to the system concerns products covered by the common agricultural policy (CAP). Given the entrenched position of the farmers' lobbies in the EEC, substantial nibbling at the edges of the CAP has never really been on the cards. However, Lomé II did produce some concessions on the fringes of the CAP and it avoided any dismantling of the sugar protocol.

The concessions apply to some vegetables such as tomatoes, carrots, onions and asparagus, and facilitate out-of-season exports to the EEC. The arrangements for beef exporters have also been improved. Under Lomé I, producers were accorded an annual quota which had to be renegotiated every year, which was not only time-consuming but nerve-racking for the producers, especially Botswana, for which beef exports contribute around half of foreign exchange earnings. Under Lomé II, the quota of 30,000 tons pa has been guaranteed for five years. Moreover, the four states concerned – Botswana, Kenya, Madagascar and Swaziland – have been given some discretion in dividing the global quota between themselves, and in carrying over and bringing forward parts of the quota from preceding and succeeding years in order to accommodate fluctuations in supply. Rum exports from the Caribbean are to benefit from slightly increased duty-free quotas on continental European markets, and an extension of promotional measures. There have also been minor improvements in the arrangements for banana exporters.

One area in which the ACP made very little progress in their demands concerns the rules of origin applied by the EEC to determine whether a consignment of goods should benefit from a Lomé trade concession. Underlying the rules of origin is the perfectly reasonable desire on the part of the EEC to prevent competitors in other industrial countries – for instance US or Japanese companies – establishing minor processing operations in the ACP which merely buy-in virtually complete manu-factured goods from their parents, affix a 'Made in Rwanda' label, and then export them duty-free to the European market. The rules of origin therefore provide that a certain minimum amount of processing (usually determined by a change of tariff heading) must occur either in the ACP or in the Nine before it can benefit from Lomé trade concessions. The complaint of the ACP is that the resulting required proportion of value added is set too high to be realistically attainable by their infant industries. In addition, the ACP have experienced problems when attempting to make goods qualify for Lomé concessions by accumulating ACP and EEC origin. They have yet to *prove* that high value added thresholds are hindering their ability to export processed goods, but there is no doubt both that the threshold tends to be high (often requiring local work to cover some 50–60 % of the value of the finished product) and that the rules are exceedingly complex, which may in itself be a non-tariff barrier. An indication of their complexity is the fact that 44 of the 111 pages of the Lomé II Convention are given over to provisions, lists and pro forma documents relating to the rules of origin.[15] The only concession made by the EEC has been to promise that the Council of Ministers would be more flexible in waiving the rules of origin in cases where an ACP country demonstrates that they inhibit industrial development. A related point concerns fish, which have duty-free access to the EEC market only if the vessels in which they are caught are at least 50 % owned and manned by ACP and EEC nationals. This requirement has angered the ACP who consider fish caught in their territorial waters to be as much a natural resource as the copper mined from beneath their soil and the cocoa harvested on top of it. The Lomé II negotiations produced no moderation of the EEC stance, and so the ACP have attached a unilateral declaration to the Council reiterating their definition of an ACP fish![16]

An important feature of the Lomé II trade régime as it affects the CAP is the negative one that arrangements for sugar producers remain unchanged. There are two main sources of sugar: cane and beet. Cane is grown in tropical climes. Beet is a temperate crop grown mainly in Europe and parts of the USA. The UK has traditionally used beet sugar to satisfy a small part of domestic demand, and has found the balance in cane imports, mainly from the Caribbean and India. Thus even in 1977/78 after UK beet production had increased following the UK's accession to the EEC, domestic beet production accounted for only 40 % of domestic consumption. Among the other members of the EEC, beet sugar has been traditionally a much more important source of supply. In 1977/78 production in the Eight accounted for 157 % of consumption Overall, the Community is more than self-sufficient in sugar, (France alone is now the second largest sugar exporter in the world, after Cuba), and the EEC surplus is tending to grow: in 1968/69 the rate of self-sufficiency for the Nine was 115 % this fell in the early to mid-1970s, but by 1977/78 it was up to 126 %.[17]

Before it joined the EEC, the UK imported cane sugar under the Commonwealth Sugar Agreement which guaranteed access and fixed prices for a quota of 1.8 million tonnes pa. On entry, an EEC sugar agreement was negotiated to provide some continuity of treatment for Commonwealth exporters. It was negotiated at the same time as Lomé I, and is annexed to the Convention as a protocol. However, it has an independent existence since it is not limited in time like Lomé and its provisions also apply to India, which is not a member of the ACP. The protocol is printed in full in the Documentary Appendix. Although the EEC undertaking is given for an indefinite period, the protocol specifies that after five years from signature it can be denounced by the contracting parties subject to two years notice, although this safeguard is said to be included purely for reasons of 'juridical security'. Moreover, the ACP have complained about the EEC's stance in the important annual negotiations over price levels, and over its interpretation of the 'force majeure' clause.[18] The protocol therefore came up on the Lomé II agenda.

From the outset, Britain's partners in the EEC have been less than enthusiastic in support of the sugar protocol since, unlike UK, they have no current need to import cane sugar. France has substantial capacity in its cane refineries and a ready source of supply of cane from French overseas departments, but these interests are heavily outweighed by those of French beet producers and processors. Moreover, since 1975 British interests have shifted towards beet as domestic production has increased under the seemingly inexorable surplus-creating logic of the CAP. The balance of domestic production and consumption in each of the Nine for 1977/78 is shown in Table 3.9. Only Italy and UK produce less than they consume. Because of this, the European beet lobby has been pushing for a cut in the quotas for sugar imports. In the event, this did not occur. The sugar protocol attached to Lomé II is identical to that appended to Lomé I except for its subsequent annexures, even to the extent of replicating article 3(3) which specifically refers to a period ending on 30 June 1975! The protocol sets the ACP sugar quota at 1,279,700 tonnes at a price to be negotiated each year. And, unlike the other trade clauses, it is not subject to the Convention's safeguards clause which empowers the EEC to suspend concessions, although the annual price negotiations give the EEC some leeway. However, as explained in Chapter 1, the real danger to the ACP sugar exporters is less that the protocol will be denounced but that its benefits will be whittled away by, for example, allowing the EEC's

Table 3.9   *Domestic sugar production and consumption in the Nine, 1977/78* ('000 tons)

Country	Production	Consumption	Self-Sufficiency (%)
France	4 300	1 900	226
Germany	2 900	2 100	138
Italy	1 200	1 500	80
UK	950	2 400	40
Netherlands	830	572	145
Benelux	728	350	208
Denmark	512	220	233
Ireland	168	150	112
Total	11 588	9 192	126

Source: Europe Information 19/79 *Sugar, the European Community and the Lomé Convention* (Commission of the European Communities, Spokesman's Group and Directorate-General for Information, Brussels) p. 4.

cane refining capacity to disappear. Further, there is pressure to link the EEC's current sugar problems to its aid programme by charging part of the levy on 'B' quota sugar to the development budget, and by restricting EEC aid and investment to sugar projects in the ACP. Ivory Coast, for example, has been persuaded to shelve EEC and French aided sugar complexes. Both of these pressures are outlined in Chapter 1.

Aid: a lot less of the same

According to EEC press releases at the end of the negotiations, the funds available under the Convention have been increased by 62% over Lomé I.[19] This figure is totally misleading. Not only does it ignore inflation and the swelling of the ACP ranks, but it also includes funds that do not qualify as aid (oda) or even as hard loans as well as some figures that are purely cosmetic. When account is taken of all these factors, the real oda per head of the ACP population has been cut by around one-fifth.

The figure of a 62% increase comes from a comparison of Eua 3,466 million available under Lomé I with Eua 7,624 million mentioned during the Lomé II negotiations (see Table 3.10). Some background information on the mechanics of EEC aid spending is required to understand Table 3.10. The EEC has two agencies for disbursing money to ldcs: the European Development Fund (EDF) which is effectively the name of a bank account administered by the European Commission's Directorate-General for Development (DG VIII); and the European Investment Bank (EIB) which is an independent body in the constellation of Community institutions. The EDF is spent in three ways: conventional projects which are appraised by DG VIII; conventional projects that are appraised by the EIB; and the trade/aid hybrid of Stabex, soon to be joined by a minerals facility. The split in responsibility between DG VIII and EIB for appraising EDF projects is undertaken theoretically on a purely sectoral basis. The EIB handles industry, services (including tourism), mining, agro-processing and some parts of infrastructure on the assumption that these sectors are more likely to sustain 'bankable' projects. DG VIII handles the rest. The EIB uses the EDF money in one of two ways. It can add a dash of cheap EDF money to a package of commercial money to subsidise interest rates by three percentage points (with the proviso that the borrower's interest rate should not be more than 8 % or less than 5 %). Or it can use the EDF money by itself as a soft loan or equity holding; what it calls "risk capital". In addition the EIB can raise commercial money in the ordinary way and lend it to an ACP state for projects that can sustain a commercial interest rate. The EDF, and hence DG VIII, on the other hand, is basically in the business of distributing grants to suitably appraised projects and controlling their execution.

In terms of the Lomé II figures in Table 3.10, the EIB is responsible for administering the Eua 685 million of loans under the Convention, the Eua 200 million of loans outside the Convention, the Eua 280 million from the

Table 3.10 *Aid and other EEC finance under Lomé I and Lomé II: Current price comparisions* (Eua million)

| | | Lomé II | |
	Lomé I	*Under the Convention*	*Outside the Convention*
EDF			
Grants	2 155	2 928	
Special loans[a]	444	504	
Risk capital[b]	94	280	
Stabex	382	550	
Minerals Facility	–	280	
Total EDF	3 076	4 542	
Delegations & sundry items			180
EIB			
Loans	390	685	200
Total	3 466	5 227	380
Grand Total		5 607	

Notes:
a – Special loans are for 40 years with 10 years grace, and an interest rate of 1 % per annum.
b – Terms of transfers determined on a case-by-case basis; transfers made by EIB.

EDF earmarked for risk capital, plus Eua 175 million out of the EDF grant allocation for subsidising interest rates.

Of the items listed in Table 3.10 under the heading 'Lomé II–under the Convention', only the Eua 4542 million allocated to the EDF counts as oda.[20] The remaining Eua 685 million of EIB loans under the Convention count as non-aid flows. The two items listed as being 'outside the Convention' require some explanation. Both arise from the EEC's efforts to get round the impasse created when the ACP rejected the aid package offered at the Easter 1979 ministerial conference. Under Lomé I the cost of running the EEC's delegations in the ACP states was a charge to the EDF. It has now been transferred to the EEC budget. Hence the Eua 180 million itemised in Table 3.10 does not represent finance available to the ACP. It is therefore misleading to lump it into the Lomé II package to produce the Eua 5,607 million figure cited so widely. However, there is a case for taking it into account when comparing the Lomé I and II deals. Although the cost of running the delegations should not be added to the Lomé II package, it should be deducted from the Lomé I EDF total of Eua 3,078 million.

The justification for including the other extra-Convention item for EIB loans is even more tenuous. The figure of Eua 200 million refers to EIB commercial lending. As noted above, the EIB can raise finance from commercial sources and lend it to commercially viable projects in the ACP. Special rules apply to such loans: the projects must be in the mining and energy sectors; they must be of mutual interest to the EEC and the ACP; and they must be approved individually by the Bank's board of governors. The EIB's power to lend in this way (under Article 18 of its statute) is in no way linked to, or limited by the Lomé Convention. It is determined solely by the supply of bankable projects on the one side, and of commercial funds on the other, and by the board of governors' views about the desirable proportion of EIB lending that should occur outside the EEC. There is nothing in the Lomé Convention requiring the EIB to lend the full Eua 200 million itemised, but neither is there anything to prevent it lending more if, for example, an attractive oil-related project were to emerge in, say, Nigeria.

Having cut through the thicket of agencies and facilities, the value of the financial provisions of Lomé II can be compared with those of Lomé I. The total for Lomé I shown in Table 3.10 is Eua 3,466 million, but from this must be deducted the cost of running the delegations, assessed by the EEC as Eua 180 million.[21] In money terms, therefore, the Eua 5,277 million under the Lomé II Convention represents a 59% increase over Lomé I. However, it is necessary to make adjustments to these figures in order to assess whether the ACP have managed to increase or maintain their aid in real terms. First, the Lomé II pledges should be deflated to a 1975 constant price basis, using the index of OECD export unit values over the period 1975–79. This shows an inflation rate of 40%. Second, the figures should be converted to an annual basis. For Lomé I, this means dividing by four, as the financial provisions took effect one year late, whereas for Lomé II the pledge covers five years. Finally, the aid pledge can also be adjusted to reflect changes in the ACP population. In 1975, this stood at 270 million. The addition of some islands to the ACP, plus natural population growth, means that even a conservative figure of 2.5 % annual growth would give a projection of 305 million for the ACP population at the end of 1979. It implies, however, that the EEC's aid pledge would have to increase by 13 % if the ACP's per capita aid is to be maintained. The results of these calculations are given in Table 3.11, which shows that on a real, annual, per capita basis the total finance available has been cut by 19 % while the EDF (the only part qualifying as oda) has been cut by 21 %. Even if the population growth is discounted, Lomé II is still around 10 % down on Lomé I.

The shares of the Nine in contributing to the Lomé II EDF (technically EDF V) are slightly different from those that applied to EDF IV. Table 3.12 shows the percentages: Germany is paying more, and is the top contributor to EDF V, while all the other members, except Denmark, are paying less.

Table 3.11 *Is Lomé II worth more than Lomé I?*

Total finance	Eua million		% change
	Lomé I	Lomé II	
At current prices	3 286	5 227	+ 59
At 1975 constant prices	3 286	3 734	+ 14
On a real annual basis	822	747	− 9
On a real annual per capita basis (Eua)	3.04	2.45	− 19
EDF only			
At current prices	2 896	4 542	+ 57
At 1975 constant prices	2 896	3 244	+ 12
On a real annual basis	724	649	− 10
On a real annual per capita basis (Eua)	2.68	2.13	− 21

Table 3.12 *Who pays for the EDF?*

	% share of:	
	EDF IV	EDF V
Germany	23.95	28.30
France	25.95	25.60
UK	18.70	18.00
Italy	12.00	11.50
Netherlands	7.95	7.40
Belgium	6.25	5.90
Denmark	2.40	2.50
Ireland	0.60	0.60
Luxembourg	0.20	0.20

Apart from the size of the financial package, the only major changes on the aid front concern Stabex and the new minerals facility. The proportion of the EDF earmarked for Stabex is unchanged, but the dependence and trigger thresholds have been reduced from 7.5 % to 6.5 %, and from 2.5 % for the least developed, island and landlocked states to 2 %, and the repayment terms for those recipients that do not qualify for grants have been softened to give a two year grace period after the market has recovered, followed by a seven year repayment period. Furthermore, the reporting rules have been changed to encourage the recipients to spend the transfers in the afflicted sectors. The ACP are now expected to submit a statement (ex ante) outlining the intended use of the money before the transfer is approved, as well as a report (ex post) within twelve months of receipt explaining how the money has been used. However, these regulations have no legal teeth. Failure to submit an ex ante statement will not delay approval of a transfer, and even if a statement is made, the ACP state is entitled to change its mind on use. Moreover, the Convention reiterates the principle that transfers are to be used freely. The purpose of the new rules is to persuade rather than to force. Only time will tell if they are successful. However, it should be borne in mind that it is inherent in the nature of free foreign exchange transfers that they are completely fungible. Experience with Stabex transfers to Amin's Uganda and Bokassa's Central African Empire during Lomé I bear witness to this painful fact.

Industrial co-operation: emphasis on energy and mining

The new minerals-related 'window' for the EDF noted above is the most significant element of a package of declarations and measures in the new Convention directed towards the energy and mining sectors. Underlying them is the Community fear that some of its sources of mineral supply are threatened by low investment in African mining ventures. The concern is not just that mineral supplies may dwindle, but that the source of supply will tend to shift away from Africa, with which the EEC is in a strong bargaining position, towards the USA, Canada and Australia, which are much stronger bargaining partners, or to third countries where other industrialised mineral users represent more powerful competition.

The details of the minerals facility, variously known as 'Minex' or 'Sysmin' (for système minérais), have still to be worked out in practice. In essence it performs two functions. First, it goes some way towards satisfying the demands of mineral exporters for an extension of Stabex in their direction; a demand made the more insistent by an unguarded promise by Chancellor Schmidt in 1978 just after the first Shaba invasion that copper would be included in Stabex. The problem for the EEC with extending Stabex treatment to minerals is that it could prove to be very expensive. If copper had been included under Lomé I, it would have absorbed the entire fund very rapidly. Stabex is clearly designed for 'soft' commodities, and the inclusion of iron ore in the heat of the Lomé I negotiations has been widely regarded as an anomaly. The second function of Minex is to provide a new, prompt, emergency resource: a fund to finance exceptional measures in times of crisis, such as Shaba.

The text of the minerals facility is presented in full in the Documentary Appendix. In the first instance, it is claimed to cover five mineral groups: copper (including associated production of cobalt), phosphates, manganese, bauxite and alumina, and tin. Calculations show, however, that no ACP countries meet the export thresholds for manganese and tin. Iron ore from existing workings will continue in Stabex for the next four years but will then be transferred to Minex.[22] There are two main differences between the schemes. First, Stabex pays out following all but the smallest earnings shortfalls. The minerals facility is only intended to provide partial compensation following major catastrophes when earnings drop below production costs. If the rules are applied rigidly only 10 ACP countries will be eligible, since the minerals should account for 15 % of total export earnings (10 % in the case of the least developed, island and landlocked states). However, it is unlikely that the rules will be applied rigidly, and herein lies the second main difference between the two systems. Stabex payments are automatic provided that the technical qualifying conditions are met. Under the minerals facility, the EEC will have considerable discretion over whether to approve a transfer. This has positive and negative implications. Negatively, an expensive claim could be simply disregarded. Positively, it means that the facility can be quick off the mark. Indeed, there is specific provision for the EEC to award an advance payment (a procedure introduced to Stabex only in 1979).

The other innovations in this field involve a quasi most-favoured nation (mfn) clause for investment codes, and an opening for the Commission to act as an "honest broker" bringing together private European capital and receptive ACP governments to promote joint mining ventures. In addition, parts of the aid and loan allocation have been earmarked for the mining and energy sectors.

The investment code arrangement was a particularly sensitive issue on both sides of the negotiating table. At the start of the negotiations some of the groups in the EEC wanted to persuade the ACP to accept an ambitious scheme whereby the Community would provide investment guarantees. Whether the ACP would have accepted this (and its corollaries) is not known, because they were never asked. They were never asked, because the EEC could not agree itself. Indeed, some officials closely involved with the negotiations claim that the EEC-ACP confrontations were more than equalled by the disputes among the Nine. The smaller EEC member states were particularly keen on community-level agreements, but Germany, France and UK were all opposed. Germany's opposition stemmed from the fact that it already has an extensive network of over 40 bilateral investment protection agreements. France and Britain do not have such an extensive network, but they opposed the move on the grounds of not wishing to lose national sovereignty over a tool for influencing the direction of foreign investment.

Because of these differences among the Nine, all that was asked of the ACP was that if they negotiate a bilateral investment code with one of the Nine, its provisions should be extended to the other eight. The ACP have agreed partially, but it is clear that the issue is a sensitive one. The relevant section of the Convention is Article 64, in which the ACP appear to accept the *right* of non-discriminatory treatment of investments as between EEC members. But in a remarkable exchange of letters between the ACP and EEC spokesmen at the time of the signing ceremony (H. B. St John and Michael O'Kennedy) this agreement is altered significantly. The letters are reproduced in full in the Documentary Appendix. They were not incorporated into the first published version of the Convention,[23] although their implications are profound. Taking Article 64 and the exchange of letters together, the ACP have agreed that they will *probably* extend mfn treatment to EEC investment codes, but they reserve their right not to do so. The mfn clause only applies between EEC members: Lomé does not require the ACP to extend to the Nine the benefits of any special deals done with, say, the USA. However, many of the ACP have a global investment code arrangement with at least one of the Nine. Under the new rules, there is the possibility that these will now be generalised to all EEC states.

The Commission's new role as 'honest broker', promoting new mining ventures, centres on Annex VIII to the Convention: joint declaration on the encouragement of mining investment. This terse, one paragraph declaration notes that

> In order to encourage European investment in mining and energy development projects promoted by the ACP states, the Community and the Member States, on the one hand, and the ACP States, on the other, pursuant to the general aims of the treatment of investments referred to in Title IV, may also conclude agreements relating to individual projects where the Community and possibly European undertakings contribute towards their financing.

There is some feeling in Brussels that real action will be slow to emerge. The Community umbrella for ACP mining and energy ventures may be no more tangible than the efforts of the joint EEC-ACP Centre for Industrial Development was for Lomé I investments from the private sector.

One final area of the negotiations, which resulted in an agreement attached to the Convention, is the treatment of migrant workers. The joint declaration (Annex XV to the Convention) is reproduced in the Documentary Appendix. It apparently guarantees ACP (and EEC) migrants who are legally employed abroad the same treatment, as regards working conditions, pay and employment-linked social security benefits, as nationals. It remains to be seen whether ACP governments have the means to enforce this.

Lomé and the wider world

The analysis so far has concentrated on the merits of the Lomé package for the ACP. But Lomé's implications are much broader than the ranks of the ACP. It is the centrepiece of EEC relations with the Third World. Some crumbs are thrown to other ldcs by the Community, but they are clearly secondary: food aid, preferential trade arrangements with quantitative limits, and some financial aid. The next chapter examines these arrangements in detail and leads to the unambiguous conclusion that the ACP are more favoured than other ldcs. It is true that the Nine have bilateral aid programmes which can be used to moderate the concentration on the ACP. But there is no inherent requirement that bilateral programmes should be used in this way, and in practice those of France and Belgium tend to reinforce the focus on the ACP.

To the extent that Lomé diverts trade and aid from one set of ldcs to another, it is divisive. Its divisiveness has been evident from the outset when the former British colonies were split into the 'associables' and 'non-associables'. And it has been given a sharper twist in 1980 in the wake of the British government's cutback in its aid programme. The Government Expenditure White Paper of March 1980[24] projects a 15% decline in British aid in the period to 1983/84. Because the government is already locked-in to a certain level of aid commitment under Lomé II, and through it other multilateral commitments, the cuts will fall most sharply on the bilateral aid programme, and the major effects will be felt by countries like India and Bangladesh.

The divisiveness of Lomé is clearly not in the interests of the ldcs that are outside the charmed circle. But is it even in the interests of the EEC? There is no consensus on this question. Clearly the key policy-makers in the Community believe that it is in the EEC's interests. Indeed some, notably the French, are fervent in their support of the Lomé concept, but others are sceptical. There are two levels to the question of the EEC's interests. First, there is the choice between concentration and globalism. Second, if the argument goes in favour of concentration, there is the question whether the ACP is the most sensible region on which to concentrate. The focus on the ACP, which effectively means Black Africa, implies a relative neglect of other regions: Latin America, or South East Asia, for example.

This is not the place to thrash out the pros and cons of the Lomé orientation. Lomé is a fact and, barring major changes, will remain a fact for the next five years. But it is necessary to point to the difference of view on the benefits of Lomé to Europe because it colours the forecast of likely developments. After the sour atmosphere in which the second Lomé Convention was signed, questions were raised about whether there would be a Lomé III. Posed in these terms the question is not very sensible. Five years in politics is a very, very long time, and prospects are unlikely to be greatly affected by the specific circumstances of the Lomé II negotiation process. The EEC Nine could be at least Ten, and possibly Twelve by the time Lomé II is up for renegotiation. But the negotiating climate will be determined by the two sides' perceptions of their own self-interest. The likelihood of the ACP's relatively favourable treatment being renewed is linked to the overall benefit the EEC derives. Perceptions of self-interest may not correspond to reality, but, as the next chapter on the impact of the EEC's enlargement argues, any delusions that the Nine may have on this score will be severely challenged over the coming years. It is possible, therefore that when Lomé II comes up for renewal the EEC will decide that it cannot afford any longer to discriminate against some non-ACP states in the developing world in which it has greater interests, whether these be economic, political or strategic.

Notes

1   Jacques Ferrandi, 'De Lomé I a Lomé II', *Marchés Tropicaux* (Paris 28 September 1979) p. 2612.
2   'Statement by the President of the Council of ACP Ministers on the occasion of the Opening of the Negotiations of the Successor Arrangement to the Lomé Convention' (ACP Group, Brussels, 24 July 1978) p. 5.
3   'Speech delivered by the President of the Council of the European Communities, on the occasion of the opening ceremony of the negotiations for the new ACP-EEC Convention' (ACP-CEE/95 e/78) p. 5. Emphasis added.
4   Not least in the latest report of the OECD's Development Assistance Committee (DAC) *Development Co-operation: 1979 Review* (Paris, November 1979), and in the report of the Brandt Commission which was made public in January 1980.
5   Nevertheless, ACP banana producers found that their access to EEC markets under Lomé I was far from unrestricted. Hence the inclusion of a 'banana protocol' (Protocol No 4) in Lomé II.
6   The World Bank *World Development Report 1979* (Washington, 1979) Table 12.
7   *Analysis of Trade between the European Community and the ACP States, 1979 Series: Trade* (Eurostat, Luxembourg 1979) Section 5.
8   *Africa Economic Digest* (London, 1 August 1980) p. 24.
9   The sugar concessions are not actually part of the Lomé Convention, but are detailed in a separate protocol; nor were they formally subject to renegotiation in 1978/79.
10 *The Courier* (Commission of the European Communities, Brussels, No. 31, March 1975) p. 20.
11 According to the OECD DAC definition.

12 Outlined in A. Hewitt 'The European Development Fund as a Development Agent: some results of EDF aid to Cameroon', *ODI Review* No 2–1979 (London) pp. 41–56.

13 *ibid.* p. 55.

14 Products covered by Stabex: the original twelve (from 1975 onwards): Cocoa beans, paste and butter; coffee beans and extracts; cotton; coconuts, coprah, coconut oil and oil-cake; groundnuts, oil and oilcakes; palm nuts and oil; tropical wood, roughly sawn or sawn lengthwise but not further processed; bananas; tea; raw sisal; iron ore, concentrates and pyrites; raw hides, skins and leather. Seven additions agreed in 1977: Ylang-ylang; gum arabic; vanilla; cloves; pyrethrum; mohair; wool.

15 These pages refer to the version of the Convention published in *The Courier* (Brussels, No. 58, November 1979).

16 Annex XLIV. 'Declaration of the ACP States on the origin of fishery products.'

17 Europe Information 19/79. *Sugar, the European Community and the Lomé Convention* (Commission of the European Communities, Spokesman's Group and Directorate-General for information, Brussels) p. 4.

18 A country's quota can be cut if it fails to deliver the full amount and if it cannot persuade the Commission that the shortfall is due to 'force majeure'.

19 See, for example, European Communities Commission Background Report, *Lomé II: Terms of the New Convention* (London, September 5 1979) p. 4.

20 And, within this, the status with regard to 'grant element' of some of the minor amounts such as risk capital is only doubtfully *oda*; the outcome would be determined by the rapidity with which the capital was reimbursed.

21 The budgetary provisions for Lomé II outside the Convention is thus identical with the element of Lomé I's EDF earmarked for delegation expenses. Since inflation is likely to mean higher money costs during the Lomé II period, this budgetary provision may well prove to be inadequate. In which case, part of the finance earmarked for EDF grants may again be diverted from developmental to administrative expenditure. Even some of the administrative costs of the home-based DG VIII, including salaries, were absorbed under this head during Lomé I.

22 Consequently existing production of iron ore exporters such as Mauretania and Sierra Leone continue for the time being to be favoured by the softer terms and conditions offered by Stabex in contrast to the Minex scheme.

23 *The Courier* (Commission of the European Communities, Brussels, No. 58, November 1979).

24 *The Government's Expenditure Plans, 1980–81 – 1983–8* (London HMSO, Cmnd 7841, 1980) pp. 24–5.

4

The Pyramid of Privilege

Philip Mishalani, Annette Robert, Christopher Stevens, Ann Weston

The Lomé Convention, described in the previous chapter, is only one of a highly complex and confusing set of commercial agreements linking the EEC with the Third World. Lomé's importance is that it sits at the apex of this pyramid of relationships. At the base are those ldcs which benefit only from the Generalised System of Preferences (GSP). In between come a set of bilateral and regional arrangements some of which provide trade concessions, while others also include an aid provision. Of course, the provisions of these agreements are only one influence on trade and financial flows, and they need not be the most decisive influence. Indeed, it is clear from the trade statistics that formal trade preferences have often been insufficient to shift the pattern of trade flows against the countervailing pressure of other factors such as overall competitiveness and the intra-firm dealings of multinationals. Nonetheless, this pyramid of agreements does provide the framework in which the other factors have to operate. Moreover, the EEC claims that its preferences are an important influence on flows. This claim should be examined against events.

It is a shifting pyramid. The countries at the top have trade preferences not only over developed countries, but also over other members of the pyramid. Hence a change in the EEC's terms with one group may affect the value of its terms with another. The ACP have complained, for instance, that their preferential access to the European market is being devalued by extensions to the GSP. Potentially the most destabilising of all the changes likely to affect the pyramid in the near future is the enlargement of the EEC. Enlargement will raise the new entrants from their current position (in Spain's case fairly near the base of the pyramid), to a commercial and financial relationship with the Nine that will naturally be significantly more favoured than even that of the ACP. This chapter therefore examines the nature and scope of the EEC's multifarious agreements with Third World countries and groups (other than Lomé) which are outlined in Table 4.1. It outlines the rationale behind them, and considers the impact on the Third World of EEC enlargement.

Table 4.1   *The Network of EEC Relations with the Third World*

Countries	Agreement
(1) African, Caribbean and Pacific countries	Lomé Convention (1980 for 5 years)
(2) Applicants to the EEC – Greece Spain Portugal	Association Agreement (1962) Preferential Trade Agreement (1970) Free Trade Agreement (1972)
(3) Maghreb countries – Algeria, Morocco, Tunisia	Preferential Trade and Cooperation Agreements (1976 for unlimited period)
(4) Mashreq countries – Egypt, Jordan, Lebanon, Syria	Preferential Trade and Cooperation Agreements (1977 for unlimited period)
(5) Other Mediterranean countries – Israel	Preferential Trade and Cooperation Agreement (1975 for unlimited period)
Yugoslavia	Preferential Trade and Cooperation Agreement (1980 for unlimited period)
Turkey, Malta, Cyprus	Association Agreements (1980, 1971 and 1973 respectively, for unlimited periods)
(6) Other ldcs (except Taiwan)	Generalised System of Preferences
(7) South Asia – Bangladesh, India, Pakistan, Sri Lanka	Non-preferential Commercial Cooperation Agreements (1976, 1974, 1976, 1975) respectively, for 5 years)
ASEAN – Indonesia, Malaysia, the Philippines, Singapore, Thailand	(One agreement, 1979 for 5 years)
Latin America – Argentina, Brazil, Mexico, Uruguay	(1972, 1974, 1976, 1975, respectively for 3 to 5 years)
(8) China Romania	Non-preferential Trade Agreements (1979 for 5 years) (1980 for 5 years)

Agreements covering trade and aid

As part of its Mediterranean policy, the EEC has preferential trade and co-operation agreements with Algeria, Morocco and Tunisia (collectively known as the Maghreb); with Egypt, Jordan, Lebanon and Syria (the Mashreq); with Israel and, most recently, with Yugoslavia. Of these, the agreements with the Maghreb are the oldest.

The Maghreb

Although both sides find it convenient to talk of the EEC's links with 'the Maghreb', in fact the EEC has separate, and different, agreements with each of the three states. The agreements with Tunisia and Morocco have a similar history, but that with Algeria is rather different. In 1957 the signatories of the Treaty of Rome declared their support for wide-ranging co-operation with Tunisia and Morocco. But negotiations did not begin formally until 1963, and only in February 1969 were agreements signed; they came into effect on 1 September 1970 for five years. In the event, the agreements were less comprehensive than had originally been hoped. They were limited to trade concessions, whereas the initial conception had been for Morocco and Tunisia to be offered associate status similar to that of the AASM,[1] with provisions for trade, financial and technical co-operation and labour relations. The slow progress of the negotiations is itself an indication of the difficulty that was experienced in reconciling the interests of EEC and Maghreb producers. Particular difficulties were encountered over wine, olive oil and citrus fruits – precisely the same products that now overshadow the issue of EEC enlargement (see below).

The main provisions of the agreements focussed on promoting the exchange of industrial goods. The EEC offered to abolish customs duties and quantitative restrictions (QRs) on all industrial goods except cork articles (which faced a tariff quota) and refined petroleum products (which faced a special safeguard clause). In return, Tunisia and Morocco undertook to dismantle the tariffs and QRs on EEC imports, except where this would lead to serious economic disruption. An association council was set up to supervise the workings of each agreement, composed of members of the European Commission and representatives of the Tunisian and Moroccan governments.

At this stage Algeria was treated differently, with a series of bilateral pacts with each of the Six instead of an agreement negotiated at Community level. When it became independent in 1962, it continued to enjoy duty-free access to the French market for all its exports, subject to certain restrictions – tariff quotas, QRs, calendar limitations and minimum import prices. (These, and other trade restrictions, are explained in the Box.) The first major change came in 1971 when wine was excluded. From Independence, Algerian exports to Germany and the Benelux countries

---

DEFINITIONS

CALENDAR LIMITATION – Restricts the times of year in which an import (usually agricultural) from certain countries is eligible for special, reduced tariffs to times when EEC supplies of that product are unable to meet EEC demand.

MINIMUM IMPORT PRICE – Goods entering the EEC at a price (including insurance and freight) below this minimum may be charged a duty or levy equal to the difference between the two.

TARIFF QUOTA – Fixes the amount of goods on which a special, reduced tariff is charged. All imports in excess of this amount must pay the normal Common External Tariff.

TARIFF CEILING – Like a tariff quota with the difference that the normal tariff is not automatically reimposed once the ceiling is exceeded but is subject to negotiation between the EEC member states.

MEMBER STATE SHARE – Fixes the amount of a tariff quota which a single member state may use. When imports to a member state exceed its share, it must reimpose the normal duty on further imports, though imports to other member states may continue at the reduced rate.

BUTOIR – Fixes the amount of a tariff quota or ceiling which any single country exporting to the EEC may use. All exports in excess of this amount must pay the full duty.

SENSITIVE PRODUCTS – Under the Generalised System of Preferences a number of products, defined as 'sensitive', face tariff quotas, member state shares and butoirs. In contrast non-sensitive products only face tariff ceilings and butoirs.

QUANTITY RESTRICTION – Fixes the amount of a product which can be imported irrespective of the tariff charged. Imports in excess of this amount are not allowed.

---

were given the same treatment as applied to EEC goods. But Italy did not offer any concessions until 1968, when Algerian goods were accorded 'most favoured nation' (mfn) treatment.

In 1976 agreements were signed with Morocco and Tunisia to supercede those of 1969 and a Community-level agreement with Algeria was made for the first time. In the early years of the 1970s, EEC thinking had changed. In 1972 the Community drew up a formal 'Mediterranean policy' recognising the strategic as well as the commercial importance of the region. This suggested that ties should be strengthened. But, at the same time, doubts were growing about the feasibility of creating a free trade area even with the Maghreb, let alone with the rest of the Mediterranean region, both because of the wide differences in level of economic development and because of pressure from the USA which objected to reverse preferences. In consequence the 1976 agreements, unlike those of 1969, were not based on reciprocity. The EEC was no doubt emboldened to accept the loss of reverse preferences by the expectation that the switch to mfn terms would not have a major effect on its exports; the EEC was, and remains, the Maghreb's most important trading partner (see Table 4.2). Another difference between the 1969 and 1976 agreements was that the latter included provisions for: EEC financial and technical assistance; encouraging contact between companies from the two sides, and EEC private investment in the Maghreb; promoting Maghreb exports; and guaranteeing Maghreb migrant workers in the EEC certain minimum conditions.

Table 4.2 *Percentage share of the EEC in the Maghreb's total trade* (by value)

		1969	1973	1978
Algeria	Imports	69.8	66.9	57.8
	Exports	81.1	64.7	38.1
Morocco	Imports	56.9	54.4	51.4
	Exports	66.1	64.6	56.4
Tunisia	Imports	58.2	62.9	65.2
	Exports	59.1	55.4	57.3

Source: UN *Yearbook of International Trade Statistics 1978* (Vol. 1).

The aid on offer is small relative to that available to the ACP (see Table 4.3). The agreements specifically provide for co-financing, so that the modest funds can be supplemented by other donors. EEC press statements made it clear that the Community had an eye on OPEC aid. The aid is intended to be used for capital projects, with emphasis on the energy sector, and technical assistance. The clauses on migrant labour guarantee to nearly one million Maghreb workers in the EEC[2] minimum pay, pensions and health provisions that are identical to those that pertain to EEC workers. In return, the Maghreb governments undertook not to discriminate against EEC citizens working in the three countries.

Despite these aid and co-operation provisions, the trade concessions remain the most important feature of the agreements, with the EEC continuing to provide duty-free access for raw materials and all industrial products that satisfy its rules of origin, albeit with the same two exceptions as before: cork and refined petroleum products. A further liberalisation occurred on 1 January 1980 when tariff ceilings were lifted from all imports from the Maghreb (and also the Mashreq).[3] The proof of

Table 4.3 *EEC Financial Pledges to the Third World*
(Eua million)

	Period	EIB loans	Loans on special terms	Grants	Other EDF	Total	Per capita per annum u.a.
Algeria	1976/81	70	19	25	—	114	1.3
Morocco	,,	56	58	39	—	130	1.4
Tunisia	,,	25	16	15	—	95	3.1
Egypt	,,	93	14	63	—	170	0.9
Jordan	,,	18	4	18	—	40	2.7
Lebanon	,,	20	2	8	—	30	2.0
Syria	,,	34	7	19	—	60	1.5
Israel	1977/81	30	—	—	—	30	1.6
Yugoslavia	1980/85	200	—	—	—	200	1.8
Cyprus	1979/83	20	4	6	—	30	10.0
Malta	1976/80	16	5	5	—	26	17.3
Turkey	1981/86	225	325	50	—	600	2.8
ACP	1980/85	685	504	2928	1110	5227	3.5
Non-associates	1976/80	—	—	423.5	—	423.5	0.05[a]
,,	1980	—	—	138.5	—	138.5	0.09[a]
,,	1980	—	—	138.5	—	138.5	0.06[b]

a excluding China and OPEC
b excluding OPEC

any trade pact is in its effect on actual trade flows. The value of the EEC's trade with each of the Maghreb countries from 1970 to 1978 is shown in the statistical appendix. The value (in current terms) of both imports and exports grew substantially over this period, but the EEC's exports grew much faster than its imports. And Table 4.2 shows that for all three countries the share of their exports going to the EEC fell between 1969 and 1978. Despite the generous duty-free provisions for industrialised goods in the agreements, there is unlikely to be a major shift in the commodity composition of Maghreb exports, at least in the short-term, because the countries lack the capacity to export industrialised goods on a large scale. Some 90 % of Algeria's total exports are crude oil while only 40 % of Morocco's and Tunisia's are non-agricultural, mainly phosphates and crude oil. Such industry as does exist – cork, petroleum products – had only limited concessions under the agreements until 1980. There are even specific provisions for restrictions on preferential treatment for motor vehicles against the day when these countries might be able to export them. More generally, each agreement contains a safeguard clause which allows the EEC to withdraw preferences on any products which the Maghreb begin to export and which cause difficulty in the EEC. This was used recently to curb imports of textile products from Morocco and Tunisia through the imposition of self-limiting agreements.

On agricultural products, the 1976 agreements are more generous than those of 1969. Reduced tariffs apply to 80 % of Morocco and Tunisia's most important agricultural exports. This compares with only 50 % under the 1969 agreement, although the cuts are still subject to certain restrictions. The products covered by the cuts, which range from 20 % to 100 %, include olive oil, wine, citrus fruits, fresh fruit, vegetables, and canned sardines, all of which are significant Moroccan and Tunisian exports to the EEC. Olive oil accounts for over 50 % of Tunisia's agricultural exports and was Morocco's fourth largest agricultural export to the EEC in 1978. The two countries benefit from a reduction in the CAP levy on imported oil, and in addition receive a proportion of the funds raised by the levy. All three countries export wine to the EEC. In 1978 the quantities involved were 12,012 tonnes from Morocco, 35,891 tonnes from Tunisia and 32,717 tonnes from Algeria.[4] Tunisia and Morocco each benefit from a duty-free tariff quota of 50,000 hectolitres for their quality wines, and an 80 % tariff reduction for table wines provided that they do not sell in Europe below the EEC minimum import price. Algeria's wine used to be exported to the EEC on a large scale, but it has had a somewhat dramatic recent history. Algerian wine exports to Europe have been falling since 1971 when the EEC's common wine market came into effect. France and Italy had very large harvests in the 1973/74 season, and as a result Algerian exports slumped from 2.7 million hectolitres in 1973 to 900,000 hectolitres in 1974. To help compensate for these losses, Algeria has been accorded a larger tariff quota for its quality wine (250,000 hectolitres in 1976 rising to 450,000 hectolitres in 1979) and an additional tariff quota for its fortified wine.

Like many of the EEC's other agreements with Third World countries and blocs, the Maghreb pacts establish a set of consultative institutions. There is a council of ministers and a committee of ambassadors to supervise the agreements and to recommend improvements. It is a moot point how effective these have been. At a formal level, they have achieved little of substance, but it could be argued that they have formed a focus for informal lobbying by the Maghreb.

The Mashreq

As part of its Mediterranean regional policy and its attempts to develop a Euro-Arab dialogue, the EEC has signed similar trade and cooperation agreements with the four Mashreq countries. Those with Egypt, Jordan and Syria were signed in 1976, but the one with Lebanon was delayed because of the country's political troubles and was not signed until 1977. The EEC now has special links with ten Arab countries: the Maghreb, Mashreq, and three ACP states (Mauretania, Somalia and Sudan). They include nearly three-quarters of the total Arab population and, more important, they have a combined trade deficit with the EEC (which totalled $3,500 million in 1975) whereas the Arab world as a whole has a substantial surplus in its trade with the EEC, largely because of oil. The EEC practice of splitting the Arab world into these camps has drawn criticism from the Arabs. The Iraqi foreign minister has complained formally to Roy Jenkins, the Commission President, and argued that the EEC should relate to the Arab League as a whole and not compartmentalise its relations between Maghreb, Mashreq and Gulf states. Nonetheless, practice has not been changed.

Table 4.4 shows the share of the EEC in the trade of the four Mashreq states. Both Lebanon and Egypt had earlier trade agreements with the EEC. The Lebanese agreement, effective from 1965, was simply a reciprocal, non-preferential trade and cooperation agreement under which each side promised the other mfn treatment, and the EEC agreed to coordinate its member states' technical assistance to Lebanon. In 1972 a preferential trade agreement was drawn up which would have given zero or reduced duties to 85 % of Lebanese industrial exports (the exceptions being plywood, petroleum and some textile products). Nearly 80 % of agricultural products would also have received tariff concessions in the EEC market. However, the agreement was never ratified because of political events in Lebanon, and the provisions of the old agreement continued until 1977.

The objective of the Egyptian agreement, effective from 1973, was to set up a free trade area. Egypt cut tariffs by up to 50 % on one third of its imports from the EEC, subject to safeguard clauses, and to quantity restrictions on some EEC products. 90 % of Egyptian industrial exports

Table 4.4   *Percentage share of the EEC in the Mashreq's total trade* (by value)

		1969	1973	1978
Egypt	Imports	30.2	29.6	38.6
	Exports	14.4	16.0	30.9
Jordan	Imports	33.1	28.2	34.8[a]
	Exports	0.0	8.5	5.9[a]
Lebanon	Imports	39.9	49.9	–
	Exports	11.4	11.6	–
Syria	Imports	31.8	37.0	35.3
	Exports	19.8	25.2	44.6

a – 1977 data

Source: UN *Yearbook of International Trade Statistics 1978* (Vol. 1)

were given preferential access to the EEC market (the major exceptions being cotton yarn and fabric, aluminium, cars and petroleum products), and over half of its agricultural exports received tariff cuts, though these were limited in the case of rice by a tariff quota, and in the case of citrus fruits by a requirement that prices had to exceed the CAP minimum.

As with Tunisia and Morocco, it soon became clear that a free trade area was not feasible: Egyptian products were unable to compete in the EEC (except for textiles and agricultural goods which had restricted access), and the Egypt-EEC trade deficit grew. In 1976, therefore, relations were reformulated, and new relations were established with Jordan and Syria following the Maghreb model. A five year aid package of Eua 270 million (see Table 4.3) was added to the trade provisions. In addition, the agreements preview other forms of co-operation between private firms in the industrial, technical and fisheries sector, and the Mashreq countries receive food aid outside the framework of the agreements. Egypt, in particular, is allocated a very substantial portion of the total food aid programme.[5]

The industrial trade concessions of the Maghreb and Mashreq agreements are very similar. The list of products subject to tariff ceilings was initially somewhat longer in the Mashreq agreements, but these differences were removed in 1980. Despite this equality of treatment, the Mashreq countries appear at first sight to be better able to take advantage of their concessions. Non-agricultural goods nominally form a much larger proportion of their exports to the EEC. In 1978 the proportion of industrial goods in the Mashreq's exports to the EEC ranged from Jordan at one end with 98 % to Lebanon at the other with 67 %. Yet, this advantage may be more apparent than real. Most of these 'industrial goods' are actually raw materials: crude oil (Syria, Egypt), raw cotton (Egypt), phosphates (Jordan), and crude animal materials (Lebanon).

Moreover, Egypt's most important processed export, cotton textiles, are actually restricted. The Mashreq's agricultural concessions are more limited than those that apply to the Maghreb, and are chiefly of interest to Egypt and, to a lesser extent, Syria and Lebanon.

Israel and Yugoslavia

The EEC's agreements with Israel and Yugoslavia have been tailormade to fit the special nature of their politically charged relationship. In 1964, the EEC offered Israel trade only on non-preferential terms but in 1970 preferential terms were agreed. In return, 60 % of EEC exports to Israel were given concessions from 1970 with the ultimate aim being to establish a free trade area. In 1976 two protocols were added to the 1970 agreement. One was on finance and previewed EIB loans but no grants (see Table 4.3). The other was more general, calling for unspecified forms of co-operation. Whereas the notion of a free trade area was abandoned with the other Mediterranean countries, it appears to be succeeding with Israel and has therefore been continued. As a result, Israel appears to be less favoured than the Mashreq in terms of formal arrangements, although in practice it is better able to take advantage of its concessions. The free trade area is restricted to industrial goods including processed agricultural products. Israeli goods therefore got the same duty-free treatment from July 1977 as did the Arabs, but in return Israel has to offer duty-free access for about 60 % of its EEC imports from January 1980, and in January 1985 to extend this to the remainder, though the date can be delayed to 1989 if necessary. All quantity restrictions must be removed by 1985. This element of reciprocity has not even allowed Israel to win more substantial agricultural concessions than those given to the Arab states. For example, although its tariff preference on citrus fruit (except lemons) is larger at 60 % than the 40 % under the 1970 EEC-Israel agreement, it is still less than the 80 % granted to Morocco, a major competitor. But the extension of preferential terms to Israel has nonetheless increased competition for many exports from the Maghreb which have consequently fallen as a share of EEC imports (e.g. Moroccan vegetables).

The political importance of the recent EEC-Yugoslavia agreement was underlined by the haste with which the EEC conceded remaining points of disagreement when the late President Tito's illness was announced at the end of 1979. The EEC had a non-preferential trade agreement with Yugoslavia dating from 1973. Negotiations to extend this into a wide-ranging co-operation agreement began in 1978. The result is an agreement that is probably more generous than any of the other Mediterranean ones. For instance, there will be more EIB loans available for Yugoslavia, though it is not known on what terms. The trade concessions will also be important given Yugoslavia's large trade deficit with the EEC. As an ldc, Yugoslav exports already enjoyed preferential treatment under the

EEC's GSP. In 1977 it was the largest GSP beneficiary, accounting for 11 % of GSP imports. However only one quarter of its total exports (33 % of its industrial exports) benefitted from the GSP as several of its industrial products were designated as 'sensitive' or 'hybrid' and often had to bear the full mfn duty. Now, 70 % of its industrial exports will be duty-free, while 29 products (13 % of industrial exports) will be subject to duty-free tariff ceilings. The remaining products, textiles and non-ferrous metals, will be covered by special arrangements. Concessions were also won on agricultural items – with tariff (or levy) reductions on a fixed amount of baby beef, tobacco and wine.

Associate Agreements

These are broadly similar to the preferential trade and co-operation agreements, with protocols covering both trade and finance. EEC tariffs on all imports from the three associated countries (Cyprus, Malta and Turkey) are being reduced in three stages. In return, and in total contrast to the Lomé Convention or the preferential agreements (with the exception of Israel), the associates are committed to reducing their tariffs and other restrictions on imports from the EEC. At the end of the final stage it is intended that all trade with the EEC will be free. This day continues to fade into the distant future as the associates are unable to meet their reciprocal obligations to the EEC. In the meantime they trade on terms worse than the ACP states and the preferred Mediterranean suppliers, particularly on agricultural products. For example, EEC imports of fresh oranges from Turkey pay 60 % of the mfn duty, but from Tunisia they pay only 20 %. The financial protocols offer a lower proportion of grants than are given to the associated ACP states or the nine preferred Mediterranean countries, but in total, *per capita*, terms Cyprus and Malta receive more assistance that any other country, even the ACP states.

In July 1980, the EEC's agreement with Turkey was renegotiated. The main changes concern migrant labour and aid. Turkish workers already in the EEC are offered an improved deal with the possibility in certain circumstances of automatic extensions to their work permits. The aid package is fixed at Ecu 600 million over five years from November 1981. Some Ecu 225 million of this is to be spent by the EIB and will attract an 8 % rate of interest. A further Ecu 50 million will be in the form of grants, and the remaining Ecu 325 million will be loans from the EEC budget, repayable over 40 years at 1 % interest. On the trade front, the EEC is reported to have promised that tariffs on Turkish agricultural exports would be removed in four stages between 1981 and 1987.

Non-preferential commercial co-operation agreements

These agreements are all based on a similar model and cover countries in South Asia (Bangladesh, India, Pakistan, Sri Lanka), Latin America

(Argentina, Brazil, Mexico, Uruguay) and China. All were established initially by the EEC negotiating with its partners individually, but these bilateral agreements are now being superceded in some cases by multilateral accords. In 1980, the five south-east Asian members of ASEAN (Indonesia, Malaysia, Philippines, Singapore and Thailand) negotiated with the EEC as a group. A similar multilateral 'framework' agreement is likely to be signed with the Andean Pact before the end of 1980, as is a bilateral one with India to supercede the existing commercial co-operation agreement. The agreements are essentially formal documents with few specific provisions. Their aim is to promote bilateral trade, not on the basis of any special concessions, but through each side offering the other mfn treatment. Indeed, so limited are the concessions that these 14 developing countries receive better treatment under the GSP than they do under the commercial co-operation agreements.

The value of the commercial agreements appears to lie in the institutions which have been set up under them – the joint committees. These provide a formal structure for discussion of trade problems. For instance ldcs may use joint committee meetings to raise the question of improvements in the GSP on products of particular interest to them. Other ldcs have no such forum. However there can be no *negotiation* on GSP even in this framework as the commercial agreements do not alter the fact that GSP is non-negotiable. More significant may be the opportunity to discuss areas of 'mutual interest'. Talks in the EEC-India committee for instance have led to an exchange of delegations from computer firms, to a visit of European farmers to India, and to advice on the quality of Indian tobacco. But these activities are frustrated because they must be financed from the small 'non-associate' aid component of the EEC's general budget as there is no aid specifically attached to any of the agreements. Moreover, where conflicting interests have emerged the committees have been unable to resolve them. This may reflect the weakness of bilateral agreements – it is too early to say whether the EEC-ASEAN agreement will be any more successful. Certainly, the Indians negotiating the new 'framework' agreement expect few significant changes, other than, perhaps, the creation of more committees for joint discussions. It is possible that this stalemate will persist as long as the 'co-operation' is one-sided. Demands for ldcs to offer something in the commercial field, if not actual tariff reciprocity, are increasing (see below) and until they are acknowledged commercial co-operation may remain a dead letter.

Aid is not an important part of these links. There is a non-associate aid budget from which these countries can benefit, but until 1981 the aid was not dealt with in the context of the commercial co-operation agreements. The 1980 ASEAN agreement incorporated a development article for the first time in any agreement between the Community and non-associated developing countries, but this has no specific allocation and merely refers to the general non-associate aid budget. The EEC's non-associate aid programme only began in 1976 with a small fund which has been increased gradually. Eua 110 million was available in 1979, all in grant form. In 1980 this was increased to Eua 138.5 million. Whereas EDF aid for the ACP is contractual and multiannual, non-associate aid is decided each year according to pressures within the Council of Ministers. It is largely the French and Italians who are unwilling to see the EEC's regionally concentrated external aid diluted by increasing assistance to other ldcs, in particular to the Indian sub-continent. As a result the non-associate aid budget is ridiculously small in per capita terms – 0.09 ua per capita in 1980 if China and OPEC are excluded, 0.06 ua if China is included – compared to the 3.5 ua per capita available for the ACP under Lomé II. Some of this discrepancy is made up by individual member states' bilateral aid programmes. For instance, India is the largest single recipient of German and British aid. But in the long run, if bilateral aid is to be replaced by EEC aid, it is important that a larger proportion is given to the non-associates. In addition to financial aid, the non-associates receive a substantial proportion of the EEC's food aid programme. As with financial aid, however, allocation is on a yearly basis and lacks continuity.

Generalised System of Preferences

The GSP was introduced in 1971 and comes up for renewal in 1981. The key feature distinguishing it from the EEC's other agreements with ldcs is that it is autonomous and non-binding. In other words the EEC, as other GSP donors, is under no legal obligation to offer GSP to ldc exports. The ldcs attempted to change this during the Tokyo Round of GATT multilateral trade negotiations by calling upon the dcs to extend the GSP for another 20 years and to pay compensation if they wanted to withdraw it. While the dcs agreed to an indefinite extension of the GSP they were only prepared to offer consultation (and not compensation) with any ldcs likely to be affected by the modification or withdrawal of GSP. However this legal weakness of the GSP is of only limited importance since even the Lomé Convention does not provide for compensation if tariff preferences are withdrawn under the general safeguard clause.

In principle the EEC's GSP offers all ldcs (except Taiwan) duty-free access for all industrial products, which is as good as the terms offered to ACP, Maghreb and Mashreq exports, and reduced duty for some 300 agricultural products, but with very few concessions on CAP products. In practice, however, the restrictions built into the GSP – tariff quotas, and ceilings, member states' shares and butoirs (see box) – mean that the terms for industrial products are a lot worse than for ACP. The EEC has tended to justify these restrictions on GSP treatment as necessary to protect the interests of ACP exporters, for instance, of canned pineapples and plywood, and of preferred Mediterranean exporters. Under article 11 of the Lomé Convention,[6] the ACP are allowed to comment on the GSP offer each year. In cases where the ACP have objected, the EEC has tended to restrict the GSP rather than maintain the GSP concession and accept ACP claims for compensation. Despite this genuflection to ACP interests, however, GSP restrictions are more often really intended to satisfy protectionist sentiments in EEC industry.

The GSP offers little trade stimulation for a number of the most important ldc exports (notably footwear, textiles), which have very small tariff quotas, or for the more competitive ldcs, whose exports exceed the butoirs. Textile products are effectively limited by quantity restrictions under the MFA. For other products facing tariff quotas, importers cannot be certain that their goods will be duty-free, and any duty reduction tends to be treated as a windfall profit. In contrast duty-free treatment has been virtually guaranteed to date for importers trading in industrial goods with ACP states (with some exceptions – see Chapter 3). The Commission is currently considering improvements to the GSP after 1980 to increase the likelihood that most exports from the less developed ldcs will be duty-free throughout the year. Yet complete tariff liberalis-ation is unlikely in the present economic climate and any improvement in the GSP will have to be on the basis of a trade-off. Some EEC industries are even demanding that imports from the more competitive ldcs pay the full mfn tariff, and that these ldcs should offer some tariff reciprocity. The European Commission has drawn up a set of guidelines which suggest a sliding scale of duty-free access without restrictions (i.e. as under the Lomé Convention) for the less developed ldcs, offset by reducing the duty-free tariff quotas in 'sensitive' goods from the most competitive ldcs. However, exactly which products and which ldcs will be the subject of lengthy negotiations between the nine member states.

The Impact of Enlargement

In January 1981 Greece is due to become the EEC's tenth member. Spain and Portugal follow suit in 1983 if everything goes according to schedule. But progress is unlikely to be according to schedule. Negotiations began with Portugal in October 1978 and with Spain in February 1979. The original timetable foresaw the period up to mid-1980 being involved with identification of the problems to be solved, to be followed by the hard bargaining. All three applicants pose problems for the developing countries. But it is Spain that is likely to cause the greatest problems, both for the EEC and for ldcs, particularly in agriculture.

The entry of Spain will increase the EEC's arable land area by 27%, and its irrigated arable land by 80%. The number of farms will rise by 30% and farming population by 28%. Moreover, while Spain will thus add substantially to agricultural supply, its 36 million consumers, with per capita incomes that are 50% lower than the EEC average, will increase consumption by only 13%. This disparity between the supply and demand effects of Spanish entry will add to the cost of intervention buying under the CAP. It has been estimated that if Spain had been a member in 1976, the EEC's agricultural spending would have risen by $1,000 million.

The EEC Commission presented its appreciation of the problems occasioned by Spanish entry in March 1980 in an optimistic report which identified solutions (see box). But it has not convinced everyone in the Nine, and on 5 June 1980, in the aftermath of the compromise over Britain's contribution to the EEC Budget, President Giscard d'Estaing expressed the view that enlargement of the Community should be delayed until the difficulties arising from the expansion of the Six to the Nine were ironed out. Current estimates are that negotiations will not get fully underway until after the French presidential elections in the summer of 1981, although preliminary talks between the two sides were due to take place in autumn 1980. Unease at the implications of enlargement are not limited to member governments. In May 1980 the purchasing manager for the Nestlé Company expressed the fears of the food manufacturing industry that raw material supplies would be disrupted to protect farmers in Greece, Spain and Portugal.[7]

Discussion of the impact of enlargement has centred on the internal problems for the Nine. But there are also major problems for the EEC's Third World trade partners. The EEC Commission has calculated that the countries most severely affected will be Tunisia, Morocco and Cyprus and, to a lesser extent, Egypt, Turkey and Israel. Table 4.5 lists the goods most likely to be affected. The Commission's report on enlargement recognises these problems and confirms that there will inevitably be adverse consequences for the trade with the Community of some developing countries. It emphasises that a solution must be found, but it does not specify the measures it considers adequate, apart from concluding that the solution cannot be of a purely commercial nature, but must include 'economic and financial instruments', for example, aid.

The impact of enlargement is likely to be felt in three areas: trade, migration and investment. Products from the new entrants will compete with goods that the EEC has in the past imported from third parties. Further, any stimulus to production in the new entrants (for example, the CAP) may result in increased competition with Third World exports in non-EEC markets. Just as goods produced by the new entrants may compete with those from the Third World, so there will be competition between migrant workers. Any reduction in demand for the services of North African migrant workers is likely to have an effect on their home countries' invisible exports and levels of domestic unemployment. The investment and plant location decisions of companies are also likely to be affected by enlargement.

The Commission's proposed remedies for agricultural problems caused by Spanish membership of the EEC

Olive Oil and Vegetable Fats

Problem: Intervention buying of olive oil will rise from Ecu 500 million to around Ecul, 200–1, 500 million because Spanish production will add to supply without there being a corresponding increase in demand. *Proposed solution*: A tax on vegetable oils and fats to shift the pattern of consumption in favour of olive oil (i.e. by making other oils relatively more expensive).

Fruit and Vegetables

Problem: Producer prices in Spain will rise on entry to conform with EEC levels and production may rise in consequence. *Proposed solution*: Market restructuring to replace the quantity restrictions currently imposed by some member states by a system of reference prices; abolish premiums on citrus fruit; reduce hothouse production in Northern Europe.

Wine

Problem: The EEC is already more than self-sufficient in wine, and Spain will add more to production than to consumption, thus swelling the wine lake.

Proposed solution: A continuation of existing measures to curb production, and taxes on competitive drinks to make them more expensive relative to wine and thus shift consumption patterns in favour of wine.

Agricultural Products

Trade competition is particularly serious for agricultural products, especially for Tunisia and Morocco. Spain currently sends some 60 % (by value) of its agricultural exports to the EEC, but the Maghreb retains a share of the market because it benefits from reduced-duty concessions on off-season imports. Once the EEC gets bigger, this advantage will disappear: the European market will probably attract a large chunk of Spain's remaining 40 % of agricultural exports, thus reducing the need for imports (see Table 4.6). Grapes, for example, will be required in only five months instead of ten at present. In addition, surplus EEC produce will

Table 4.5 *EEC imports likely to be affected by enlargement; 1977 imports by product from the Arab League and from the Applicant States*

	Value of total imports '000 Eua	% shares					
		Dev. countries	Arab League	Spain	Portugal	Greece	Total Applicant States
Fresh vegetables	1 450 618	62.4	12.3	13.4	0.1	2.4	5.9
(Tomatoes)	203 078	76.4	35.4	19.0	–	–	19.0
(Potatoes)	250 979	54.0	21.1	18.4	–	7.4	25.8
(Legumes)	200 991	44.3	12.0	3.1	–	0.3	3.4
(Other vegetables)	290 215	41.8	10.7	29.5	–	4.9	34.4
Fresh fruit	2 361 179	48.9	6.4	21.8	0.3	4.1	26.2
(Oranges)	474 684	36.9	11.4	40.6	–	2.0	42.6
(Tangerines)	217 906	26.8	25.6	72.0	–	–	72.0
(Stone fruit)	94 329	4.5	2.5	15.6	–	64.1	79.7
(Nuts)	297 165	7.2	1.9	13.6	1.9	–	15.5
Olive oil	150 163	54.2	53.3	28.7	0.1	2.5	31.3

	Value of total imports '000 Eua	% shares					
		Dev. countries	Arab League	Spain	Portugal	Greece	Total Applicant States
Prepared vegetables	515 902	35.1	10.7	18.4	4.7	10.3	33.4
Prepared fruit	742 125	39.7	3.2	11.1	–	7.8	18.9
Wine	350 897	10.3	7.1	44.8	22.9	3.8	71.5
Fresh fish	834 367	27.6	2.6	6.0	0.3	0.7	7.0
Preserved fish	434 481	37.2	5.5	3.9	6.5	0.4	10.8
Petroleum products	3 712 985	32.0	15.2	1.6	–	2.0	3.6
Clothing	4 881 717	53.4	3.8	2.5	2.2	8.0	12.7
Textiles	4 083 463	37.6	3.0	3.4	4.0	5.0	12.4
Non-electrical machines	10 031 930	3.8	0.6	3.6	0.4	0.1	4.1
Electrical machines	7 074 344	12.1	0.5	2.6	1.4	0.2	4.2
Transport equipment	6 240 232	3.6	0.4	12.2	0.1	0.2	12.5
Iron & steel	3 773 307	7.8	0.3	9.4	0.3	0.8	10.5
Aluminium	1 076 268	9.5	2.3	0.1	–	7.0	7.1
Phosph. anhyd. and acids	55 652	94.0	81.4	3.0	–	–	3.0
Phosphatic fertilizers	72 541	69.4	55.7	0.4	1.1	–	1.5
Footwear	750 367	35.2	1.5	20.3	3.3	3.2	26.8
Travel goods	238 105	64.3	3.2	6.8	0.2	0.4	7.4

Source: Eurostat, EC Trade with the ACP States and the South Mediterranean States No. 1–1980.

probably be exported, possibly at subsidised prices, increasing competition in third markets.

To soften the impact, the Commission has recommended a seven to ten year transition period for Spain. This compares with the transition period negotiated with Greece of five years for reducing tariffs and seven years before workers get full freedom of movement. While the transitional period *may* defer the impact on third parties, it will not remove it. Moreover, this deferral is not guaranteed. It is clear that if negotiations with Spain proceed, they will be extremely tough. There will be strong pressure on the EEC negotiators to make whatever concessions are necessary at the expense of third party exports rather than at the expense of domestic cut-backs or tax changes.

Table 4.6   *Rate of Self-supply of the EEC(9) and the EEC(12) for leading Mediterranean agricultural products and most affected Maghreb-Mashreq countries.*[a]

	EEC(9) %	EEC(12)[b] %	Maghreb-Mashreq countries concerned
Fresh and processed vegetables	92	100	All
Fresh fruit (excl. citrus)	77	–	All
Fresh and processed fruit	78	95	All
Potatoes	98	100	Morocco, Egypt
Tomatoes	93	99	Morocco
Oranges	47	86	Morocco, Tunisia Algeria
Mandarins and other small fruit	40	96	Morocco, Tunisia Algeria
Wine	108	112	Tunisia, Morocco
Olive Oil	85	100	Tunisia, Morocco

a – All figures are for the late 1970s, 1976–78.

b – This is the projected self-supply at the current production level.

Source: EEC, The Agricultural Situation in the Community, 1979 Report; Brussels-Luxembourg, 1980.
    Europe, No. 2707, Brussels-Luxembourg, 27 June 1979.

The Commission forecasts a 200,000 tonne olive oil surplus following Spain's entry. It proposes encouraging consumers to switch to olive oil by taxing other vegetable oils, which will not be popular with consumers and suppliers of other oils. In the haggling that will result, the Maghreb's olive oil exports will be a natural target. In 1978, the EEC's vegetable oil imports totalled Ecu 41.5 million ($58.9 million) from Tunisia and Ecu 4.9 million ($6.9 million) from Morocco, representing about half their total vegetable oil exports. Olive oil production has also been expanded in both countries, partly because of the EEC trade concessions. Between 1978/79 and 1979/80 Moroccan production more than doubled from 20,000 to 50,000 tonnes. In Tunisia, an olive cultivation programme caused a threefold rise in production from the mid-1960s to the mid-1970s.

The EEC is already more than self sufficient in wine. Spanish production (22 million hectolitres in 1977) threatens to add some 15 % to the EEC's wine output. At present only 39 % (by volume) of Spanish exports go to the EEC; after enlargement this proportion will rise. The Commission's proposal is to boost consumption by reducing taxes in the UK, Belgium, the Netherlands and Denmark that make wine expensive relative to other drinks. As with vegetable oil, these proposals are unlikely to be accepted without question and curbing imports may be mooted.

At a time when the EEC is complaining about oil prices and talking about saving energy it seems incredible that imports of vegetables such as tomatoes from the south Mediterranean should be restricted while north European hothouses continue business. In 1978 Spain produced 215,000 tonnes of tomatoes, 5 % of total EEC production. The Commission has proposed that the increase in supply of tomatoes and other vegetables be compensated by a cut in hothouse production. But the Maghreb countries fear their exports may be squeezed instead. Table 4.7 lists the more important vegetables. The EEC's fruit and vegetable imports in 1978 totalled Ecu 27 million ($38.3 million) from Tunisia, Ecu 16 million ($22.7 million) from Algeria and Ecu 280 million ($397.4 million), or one third of its total imports, from Morocco.

Although the Maghreb is probably the most vulnerable Third World region on agricultural trade, the impact of enlargement will also be felt elsewhere. All vegetable oil exporting countries, for instance, are potentially liable to be affected by EEC moves to accommodate the increased supply of olive oil. The most important suppliers of vegetable oils are Malaysia, Philippines, Senegal, Argentina, and Indonesia. In the case of Malaysia, the share of vegetable oils in total exports was 15.3 % in 1978. The other Mediterranean countries (and their agricultural products) likely to be affected are Cyprus (potatoes, citrus fruit, wine), Malta (tinned vegetables and fruits), Israel (oranges, tinned fruit, fresh and tinned vegetables) and Egypt (potatoes, onions, fresh and preserved rice). The non-Mediterranean countries that compete with the candidates' vegetable exports are Argentina, Indonesia and Chile. For fruits, Martinique, Argentina, Peru, Chile, Colombia, Jamaica, and Brazil compete with all three candidates in the European market for pears, apples, oranges, mandarins and grapes (fresh and dried). On tobacco, it is Greece that poses the main problem. Competition will be felt not only in the Maghreb and Mashreq, but also by Brazil, India, Malawi, Tanzania, Zimbabwe and South Korea.

Table 4.7 *Country rank as supplier of selected vegetables to the EEC by descending order of value (1978)*

Rank	New Potatoes 1 Jan – 15 May	New Potatoes 16 May – 30 June	Beans[a] 1 Oct – 30 June	Onions[b]	Garlic	Onions[c]	Lentils[d]	Preserved Cucumbers and Gherkins	Preserved Capers	Tomatoes 1 Nov – 14 May	Tomatoes 15 May – 31 Oct
1st	Italy	Italy	Spain	Netherlands	Italy	U.S.A.	Argentina	Spain	Morocco	Canary Islands	Netherlands
2nd	Egypt	Cyprus	Italy	Spain	Argentina	Egypt	Turkey	Italy	Spain	Netherlands	Morocco
3rd	Spain	Spain	Senegal	Italy	Spain	Rumania	U.S.A.	Netherlands	Algeria	Spain	Belgium Lux'bourg
4th	Morocco	France	Kenya	Israel	France	Hungary	Lebanon	Morocco	Tunisia	Morocco	Spain
5th	Canary Islands	Greece	Egypt	Egypt	Mexico	Netherlands	Spain	Yugoslavia		U.K.	Italy
6th	Cyprus	Egypt	France		Egypt	France	Chile				
7th		Algeria	Morocco			F.R. Germany					
8th						Syria					

a – phaseolus   b – other than sets   c – dried, dehydrated or evaporated   d – dried

Source: From data in Eurostat, NIMEXE – 1978, A.

Industrial Products

The impact of enlargement on trade in industrial products will be felt in a wide range of developing countries from the Far Eastern newly industrialising countries, to Malta, Israel and Yugoslavia. For the Maghreb and Mashreq the most vulnerable sectors are textiles, clothing and footwear, and the most vulnerable countries are Morocco, Tunisia, Malta, Israel, Cyprus and Egypt. Other likely affected sectors (and countries) are cork products (Morocco, Tunisia, Algeria), inorganic chemicals and fertilisers (Morocco, Tunisia, Israel), mats, tapestries and various fabrics (Morocco, Tunisia, Egypt), iron and steel products (Algeria), aluminium products (Egypt), papermaking material (Morocco, Algeria, Tunisia), and hides, skins and leather (Lebanon).

Egypt and Greece are currently competitive suppliers of textiles to the EEC. Greece's textile exports to the EEC are much larger than Egypt's (Eua 509.5 million against Eua 8.1 million in 1978), and form a much higher proportion of its total exports to the EEC (29.6 % against 0.85 % in the same year). Despite these small percentages, Egyptian textile exports are critically important for its industrial sector, and are closely linked to the agricultural sector. Textile exports from both countries to the EEC have been quota restricted, and both have requested increased quotas.

Similarly, Morocco and Tunisia are in direct competition with the new entrants in fabrics, textiles, clothing, processed food and cork. Tunisia, for example, accounted for 15 % of the Mediterranean region's 1978 exports of clothing[8] to the EEC, compared with a 20 % share for Greece, and only 9 % for Spain. Similarly, Morocco accounted for 31 % of the Mediterranean region's 1978 exports of the trade category carpets, mats, tapestries, fabrics and industrial textiles[9], virtually the same proportion as accounted for by Greece and Spain put together. Non-Mediterranean competitors on textiles include Hong Kong (with textiles representing 48 % of its total exports in 1978), South Korea (35 %), Taiwan, India and Singapore. For footwear, South Korea, Taiwan, Brazil and Hong Kong may suffer from trade diversion.

The actual impact of enlargement on third party trade in industrial products is less easy to predict because the EEC does not have a common industrial policy to match the all-embracing protectionism of the CAP and, as Chapter 2 argues, it is unlikely to acquire one. Moreover, many of the preferential agreements described in the first part of this chapter provide, in theory, free access to the EEC market for industrial goods. But, as has been noted, access is in practice circumscribed to restrain certain exports that would embarrass EEC industry even though these are often precisely the commodities in which the EEC's trade partners have a comparative advantage and which they want to expand. Furthermore, while there is no comprehensive common industrial policy, there does already exist a highly restrictive MFA limiting trade in clothing and textiles, and restrictions on trade in footwear are spreading. Whereas the

impact on agricultural trade diversion is likely to be felt immediately the
EEC expands, the impact on industrial trade will occur more slowly as the
shift in the balance of power inside the EEC leads it to adopt more
restrictionist trade policies.

Notes

1   The AASM were the ex-colonies of France, Belgium and Italy in Africa
    linked to the EEC under the Yaoundé conventions.
2   500,000 from Algeria, 200,000 from Morocco, 200,000 from Tunisia.
3   This move does not affect QRs, nor does it lessen the restraints on exports of
    textiles from Egypt, Morocco and Tunisia under the Multifibre Agreement
    and of cotton yarn under an informal restraint that is negotiated annually.
4   By comparison, Cyprus exported 22,919 tonnes to the EEC in 1978.
5   In 1980, the Commission's proposed allocation of cereal food aid to Egypt
    was 100,000 tons, or 20% of its proposed total direct food aid in cereals.
6   Article 16 of Lomé II.
7   *Financial Times* (London, 30 May 1980).
8   Falling under Chapter 61 of the CCT.
9   Falling under Chapter 58 of the CCT.

5
Energy

The Western economic summit held in Venice in June 1980 identified energy as the key challenge. The energy issue links North and South in many ways. The Maghreb and Mashreq agreements described in the previous chapter exist against the background of the Euro-Arab dialogue. OPEC countries have been an important stimulus to formal North–South dialogue: their pressure was instrumental in launching the Paris CIEC which began in December 1975 and is the progenitor of the Global Negotiations due to begin in January 1981. On another level, North and South are linked in a competitive relationship for available energy supplies. Oil importing developing countries have a direct interest in energy saving measures adopted by the North. Similarly, oil importing industrialised countries have a direct interest in measures to increase energy supply in developing countries.

This chapter examines three aspects of the energy relationship between the non-oil producing developing countries and the North in general and the EEC in particular. The first section deals with EEC energy policies and shows how the Community's current energy policies make it unlikely that the rate of increase in oil prices will slow down significantly. It argues that the most important aspect of EEC-Third World relations over energy concerns the former's role in recycling petrodollars. It also argues for the EEC to provide aid to develop the Third World's oil potential. These two points are taken up in the second and third sections. The second section is devoted to the role of the Eurocurrency market in financing the foreign exchange needs of developing countries. The Europe-based banks are not the only vehicles are recycling, but the conventional wisdom is that they played a major role in recycling to developing countries after the 1973–74 oil price rise. It examines this conventional wisdom critically, and finds it wanting. The third section analyses the EEC's extensive energy aid programme. Lomé II gives great emphasis to an expansion of aid to the energy sector of the ACP. But who benefits from the sort of aid that the EEC is able and willing to provide? Is it the majority of the population in recipient countries? Or is it the small urban minority who benefit from conventional systems? Or, yet again, is it really the Europe-based exporters of technology? This section examines the energy aid programme in the light of these questions.

Energy Policies in the EEC and their Impact on the Third World*

Peter R. Odell

Introduction

Throughout most of the period of its modern economic development energy played a very minor role in Western Europe's relationships with what is now known as the Third World. Europe's development was coal-based and the coal was an indigenous product so that the countries of Western Europe did not have to scour the world for their supplies of energy, as they did in respect of foodstuffs and raw materials for the growing populations and their expanding industry.

It was only after 1957 (see Table 5.1) that the use of indigenous coal started to decline – first relatively to the use of other energy sources and then absolutely as the coal industry in Western Europe was undermined by the rapidly rising quantities of imported oil brought in under the aegis of the international oil companies. The successes of these companies in locating very large reserves of low cost oil in areas such as the Middle East and north and west Africa, and their ability to operate so effectively, with so little return to the producing countries (a function of European and American political control), enabled them to supply Western Europe with the rapidly increasing volumes of oil which it needed to sustain its vigorous post-1966 economic growth and its increasingly mobile population. In doing so, the oil companies undermined the economic viability of the coal industry in most of Western Europe. In a period of rising real wages the coal industry, with its high labour cost component, was unable to meet the competition from decreasing real cost oil which in 1970, as shown in Fig. 5.1, cost only 40 % as much as in 1950.

Because the United States restricted oil imports after 1959 in order to protect its domestic energy industries, it was essentially Western Europe and Japan which sustained the massive expansion of the oil industries of the OPEC countries. In the short term this was an exploitative relationship, as the oil exporters' terms of trade vis à vis the oil importers' worsened. But in the longer term the way in which all European countries, to a greater or lesser extent, decided to run such open energy economies was a major factor in OPEC's recent political strength and its ability to push up the real price of oil to ten times its level of less than a decade ago (See Fig. 1).

* Copyright © 1981 by Peter R. Odell.

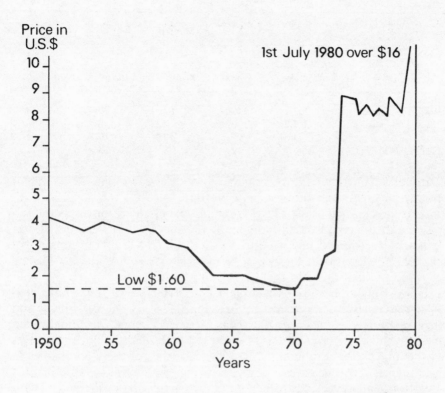

Figure 5.1   *The Price of Oil 1950–80* (in constant 1974 prices)

A further aspect of this openness has been the decline in the hitherto important differences of policy between those EEC member states that produce coal on a significant scale, and those that do not. The coal producers, notably UK and France, and to a lesser extent Belgium and Germany, have tended to oppose coal imports in order to protect their domestic industries. However, such opposition is now restricted to particular groups with vested interests, such as coal industry management and unions.

Relationships with the Oil Exporters since 1973

By 1972, oil was dominant in all Western European countries' economies, with the exception of the Netherlands where indigenous natural gas use had expanded very quickly over the previous few years. OPEC's assertion since then of its ability to control the supply and price of oil has thus been a traumatic economic and political experience for Western Europe. This has been reflected in both external relationships and in internal energy policy developments. Externally, the EEC has had to build appropriate

Table 5.1 *Energy Use in Selected West European Countries 1937–1972*

Year	Energy use	United Kingdom	West Germany	France	Italy	The Netherlands
				Country		
1937	Total mtce[a]	202	142	82	20	15
	Tons capita	4.3	3.0	2.1	0.7	1.8
	,, Coal	*94*	*97*	*89*	*70*	*87*
	,, Oil	6	2	8	18	13
	,, Gas	–	–	–	–	–
	,, Other[b]	–	1	3	12	–
1952	Total mtce[a]	232	145	89	25	22
	Tons capita	4.6	2.9	2.1	0.6	2.1
	,, Coal	*90*	*95*	*79*	*43*	*78*
	,, Oil	10	4	18	35	12
	,, Gas	–	–	–	8	–
	,, Other[b]	–	1	3	15	–
1957	Total mtce[a]	247	186	111	44	28
	Tons capita	4.8	3.5	2.5	0.9	2.5
	,, Coal	*85*	*88*	*72*	*28*	*63*
	,, Oil	15	11	25	48	36
	,, Gas	–	–	1	15	1
	,, Other[b]	–	1	3	9	–
1962	Total mtce[a]	265	221	122	71	35
	Tons capita	4.9	3.9	2.6	1.4	2.6
	,, Coal	*72*	*71*	*58*	18	47
	,, Oil	28	27	33	*62*	*51*
	,, Gas	–	1	5	13	2
	,, Other[b]	–	1	4	8	–
1967	Total mtce[a]	276	251	154	112	47
	Tons capita	5.0	4.2	3.1	2.1	3.7
	,, Coal	*59*	*51*	40	12	25
	,, Oil	39	46	*50*	*1*	*53*
	,, Gas	1	3	6	11	17
	,, Other[b]	1	1	4	6	–
1972	Total mtce[a]	302	333	215	152	76
	Tons capita	5.4	5.4	4.2	2.8	5.7
	,, Coal	40	35	21	7	6
	,, Oil	*46*	*52*	*66*	*75*	36
	,, Gas	12	11	10	14	*59*
	,, Other[b]	2	2	4	4	–

Source: Based on U.N. Energy Statistics Series J.

Notes: a – millions tons coal equivalent.

b – mainly hydro-electricity converted to coal equivalent on heat value basis of the output. 1972 figures also include some nuclear power converted on the same basis.

Most important energy source in each country for each year in italics.

diplomatic bridges to the main oil exporting countries as a means of trying to assure necessary supplies of oil. This has certainly included a re-evaluation of attitudes to the Arab/Israeli conflict as well as less tangible developments such as changed views of the Arab world in general. Though the EEC as a whole has by no means accepted the French geo-political concept of the Middle East as a natural extension of Western Europe, it has certainly taken a very much more positive view of its relations with the oil-rich region, both for reasons of oil supply and, almost equally important, because the oil exporting countries have, over the last decade, represented the most important growth area for Western European exports of both capital and consumer goods. Details of these trade relationships are given in Chapter 4. Inter-dependence is now of the essence particularly as the EEC does not really see an alternative to continuing large Western European imports of OPEC oil.

This does not mean, however, that energy policies have not been changed in response to the success of OPEC. The earlier low-cost energy emphasis has, of necessity, been dropped and has been replaced by a belief in the efficacy of the pricing mechanism as the means of cutting energy demand. This has had positive results over the last few years but a more important component in the EEC's now relatively stable use of energy is the lack of economic growth and rising unemployment. Unhappily, there are gaps in the use of the pricing mechanism – particularly in respect of motor gasoline on which governments have hesitated to maintain the previous levels of taxation (relative to pre-tax prices) and there are also institutional restraints on the effects of price on demand as, for example, in respect of the widespread use (and abuse) of 'company cars'. Moreover, neither the EEC nor individual governments have been willing to introduce serious regulatory devices for controlling the use of energy, so that demand remains higher than it need be.

These limitations on demand constraint have been accompanied by a much less than emphatic pursuit of increasing indigenous energy production as an alternative to OPEC oil. The Western European coal industry has so far been unable to reverse its long period of decline and the outlook for a major resurgence in coal production is poor. Nuclear power, in which the EEC placed so much faith and to which it gave so much attention in its future energy supply reviews in the mid-1970s, has been held up for both economic and environmental reasons and will probably make a smaller contribution than is still supposed to energy supply over the next 10 to 20 years. So-called alternative energies are neither easy to introduce into systems which were not designed for them, nor have they been supported very positively by governments whose energy research funds have largely been channelled towards nuclear power. The main gap on the supply side in the EEC arises from the under-performance of Western Europe in producing oil and gas, and in under-evaluation of their potential. Though the North Sea oil and gas province has been opened up quickly, there are major institutional and nationalistic constraints on its development and its prospects for limiting oil imports have thus been under-evaluated. Moreover, the Western Europe offshore contains many prospective areas for future oil and gas production but unhappily the level of activity and the degree to which it is encouraged remains at a relatively low ebb. Thus dependence on oil imports from OPEC countries remains higher than it need be and, as a result, the influence of OPEC countries on EEC policies and attitudes is further extended.

Relationships with the rest of the Third World

The most important aspect of EEC/non-OPEC Third World relationships over energy is an indirect one: it is the involvement of the EEC countries in the financing required by a large number of Third World countries as a consequence of the high price of imported oil. This is covered in the second section of this chapter, while the third section deals with the question of EEC energy aid to Third World countries.

In as far as EEC attention has been concerned exclusively with the financial aspects of the energy problem, the concern is for the consequences of the problem rather than with action which would mitigate the problem itself. In the short term nothing would assist the non-oil producing Third World countries more than the creation of conditions in which the price of oil stopped rising; except, of course, the creation of a situation in which its price actually fell. Unhappily, the EEC's energy policy is not designed to achieve such a result basically because it would require a controlled and regulated use of oil as a means of bringing demand some 20% to 25% below present levels. It would also necessitate maximising indigenous production of oil, gas and other sources of energy. Neither of these objectives are being pursued and in their absence the pressure of demand on OPEC oil serves to ensure the upward pressure on prices: a general situation which is exacerbated from time to time by the competitive bidding for oil supplies by the industrialised nations, including those of the EEC, in periods when supplies are temporarily affected by political or other problems in one or other of the main exporting countries. There is, moreover, one other factor – probably of growing importance – which persuades some EEC countries to avoid policies which would weaken the oil market, viz. protection of the high cost production of oil from, for example, parts of the North Sea and, even more important, the protection of investment in other energy sources – notably nuclear power which could not compete over a very extensive range of energy demands were the oil price to weaken. Despite the modest success so far in respect of nuclear power, many EEC countries, notably France, West Germany and Italy, are in the process of tying their energy futures to nuclear power so providing a circumstance in which the prospects for a fall in the real price of oil are made even more remote. Moreover, this nuclear power policy leads to one further adverse energy development for the Third World countries. This is the attempt by the nuclear power station manufacturing countries, including those in the EEC, to sell turnkey nuclear projects to the Third World in an effort to achieve appropriate economies of scale in their manufacture. In both technical and economic terms such energy technology is the most inappropriate imaginable for the poor countries of the world; yet, unhappily, it seems likely to develop as the EEC's most important contribution by far to the expansion of energy producing capacity in the Third World. The sale of nuclear plant is the most striking example of a bias in the EEC's energy technology transfers to the Third World that are examined in more detail in the third section.

This emphasis is the more unfortunate, because in the medium to long term both sides have an interest in increasing world energy supply by exploiting the Third World's huge potential for oil and gas. For the period from the mid-1980s to the end of the first quarter of the next century, the world's most significant energy potential is to be found in the many unexplored petroliferous regions of the Third World. These areas are relatively neglected because the international oil companies have not seen it to be in their interests to explore and develop them. In recent times, the companies have become decreasingly acceptable in many Third World countries, and in consequence they have largely written off these parts of the world as regions in which they are prepared to risk their investments. The implications of this serious geographical mismatch are two-fold.

First the international oil companies have written down, or even written off, most of the developing countries as potentially major oil producers. They have, indeed, failed even to update their evaluations of these regions' potential as ideas change on the patterns of oil and gas occurrence and in the light of rapidly developing geological knowledge. This is clearly demonstrated in Table 5.2 in which the companies' outdated ideas of the Third World as a habitat for oil are compared with very recent figures by others with a high and continuing interest in the hydrocarbon resources of the developing countries. Note, as an example, how ridiculous the oil company's views on the potential resources of Latin America look in the light of recent events in Mexico. That single country's proven, probable and possible reserves in themselves are now approaching the oil industry's ultimate figure for the whole of the continent, whilst Mexico's ultimate resources possibly exceed the Latin American total figure by a factor of two to three.

An understatement of the Third World's potential is, of course, justifiable from the companies' point of view. But the fact that we have institutions which, by their present nature, cannot find and develop most of the world's oil resources does not mean that they can never be exploited. Revised or entirely new institutional arrangements for tackling the oil and gas opportunities offered by the currently under-explored

Table 5.2   *Estimates of the Ultimate Oil Resources of the Third World* (in bbls $\times 10^9$)

	Oil Industry Views[a]	Grossling (U.S.G.S.)[b]	Min. of Geology USSR[c]
Latin America	150–230	490–1225	620
Africa	120–170	470–1200	730
South/S. E. Asia	55– 80	130– 325	660
Total	325–480	1090–2750	2010

Sources: a — Based on figures in R. Nehring, *Giant Oil fields and World Oil Resources*, Rand, Sante Monica, June 1978. Table on p. 88 adjusted to give comparable geographical coverage with (b) and (c). Nehring also states (p. 88) that his figures are 'roughly similar' for these regions to those published elsewhere by oil industry observers.

  b — B. F. Grossling (USGS), 'In Search of a Probabilistic Model of Petroleum Resources Assessment' in *Energy Resources*, M. Grenon, Ed., I.I.A.S.A., 1976.

  c — Visotsky et al, Ministry of Geology, Moscow, 'Petroleum Potential of the Sedimentary Basins in the Developing Countries'. *ibid*.

countries of the Third World can be created.

A second and, arguably, an even more important implication is related to the availability of the management and technological expertise and of the financial resources which are required for major oil developments. 90 % or thereabouts of such financial and human resources exist within, or are exclusively available to, the international oil companies and a small number of other entities – especially in the United States. As a consequence the possibilities for the development of the oil and gas resources of the Third World are severely limited. Local state oil companies, or even state oil entities from other parts of the World, are not an adequate substitute, especially in managerial and technological terms, for the private sector oil companies, basically because of the contrast in size and in length of experience between the two sorts of entities.

This institutionalised dichotomy between those world regions with prospects for large scale oil developments, on the one hand, and on the other, the non-availability to these regions of the resources required to develop them, constitutes what appears to be the main barrier to the rapid geographical diversification of world oil reserves and the development of an enhanced supply potential. Moreover, the continuation of the present situation means, inevitably, that scarce capital and managerial resources for oil and gas exploitation will be used in relatively low-rates-of-return ventures in 'safe' countries, rather than in finding and producing the lowest cost oil and gas in parts of the Third World.

There has been some recognition of the need for geographical diversification. President Carter, in his 'Energy Address to the Nation', 1979, commented, 'there are several potentially abundant . . . sources of foreign oil and gas that have not yet been fully explored or developed . . . The Administration is developing a broader international strategy for increasing . . . exploration in these areas'. The World Bank has launched a modest programme for investments in oil production in Third World countries, involving some $450 million over five years. Though small in relation to the opportunities and the needs, it does, nevertheless, represent a major breakthrough in that the World Bank for many years refused to invest in oil-related activities at all. It could also be the means whereby private risk capital is attracted to the ventures sponsored by the World Bank. Some of the major oil companies – including Exxon, Gulf and Shell – have already made it known that they see good opportunities for productive investment in oil developments in such countries and that they would welcome suggestions as to how they might become involved so that the political problems and the high risks associated with such projects can be minimised. Finally, some of the Third World countries themselves now appear to be more willing to reconsider their previous hostility to involvement by the international oil companies, providing they can be assured of the effective depoliticisation of the companies.

So far, the EEC has shown little interest in such avenues, despite its efforts in relation to minerals and its energy programme described in the third section of the chapter. In investment terms what appears to be needed for energy-related development in the Third World is an availability of up to $8000 million per year most of which would go for at least a decade into the oil and gas sectors. One possible strategy involves an intergovernmental agency, embracing both OECD and OPEC, and the utilisation of the expertise of the international oil companies to ensure the technical and the commercial success of the schemes. The world banking industry with its close connections with the international oil industry might also be involved. Alternatively, a more radical approach might be considered more appropriate. What is certain is that various options need to be examined so that a viable and acceptable solution to the opportunity offered to the future of the international economic system by these developable, but so far unattainable, oil and gas resources of the developing world can be found.

Eurocurrency Market Recycling of OPEC Surpluses to Developing Countries: Fact or Myth?

Tony Killick

The oil crisis and the growth of the Eurocurrency market

Prior to 1973–74, the global balance of payments (summarised in Table 5.3) was fairly settled into a pattern in which the Western industrial nations (dcs), considered as a group, earned substantial current surpluses, the non-oil exporting developing countries (ldcs) ran current deficits of a similar size and oil exporting countries earned surpluses which were small in global terms. Considered at this admittedly high level of aggregation, the main task of the international financial system was to effect the necessary transfers from dcs to ldcs so as to finance this global imbalance. Aid and direct investments by multinational corporations were the chief vehicles for this and, although there was much controversy about the adequacy of the aid flows and about the merits of direct investment, few questioned the capacity of existing institutions to handle the capital flows in question. International ldc borrowing from commercial banks was modest.

This pattern of surpluses and deficits was, however, transformed by the discovery and exploitation by OPEC of its formidable monopoly powers

Table 5.3 *Payments Balances on Current Account, Selected Periods in 1971–80*[a]

| | (US $ billion; annual averages) | | | |
	1971–73	*1974–77*	*1978*	*1979–80*[b]
Developed countries[c]	+11	− 2	+31	−31
Major oil exporting countries	+ 3	+44	+ 5	+92
Non-oil developing countries	− 9	−34	−36	−62

Sources: IMF *Annual Reports;* IMF *Survey,* 25 June 1980.

Notes: a — Figures relate to balances on current account excluding public transfers, for IMF members only, thus excluding most centrally planned economies.

b — Forecasts.

c — Industrial countries and more developed primary producing countries.

at the end of 1973, and the manifold repercussions of this on the world economy. As can be seen from Table 5.3, the oil exporters earned surpluses in 1974–75 of a size quite unprecedented in earlier years. To a remarkable extent, however, the dcs weathered this storm: they were pushed into deficit in 1974 but bounced back with large surpluses in 1975 and 1978, and were successful in avoiding persistant large deficits. Viewing the world as a whole, surpluses in some countries must give rise to counterpart deficits elsewhere[1] and the table shows that these were largely incurred by the ldcs, whose deficits nearly quadrupled in nominal value after 1973.

The non-oil developing countries were, of course, hit by the higher cost of imported oil but they were protected from the worst effects of this because their economic structures are less dependent on oil than those of the dcs (in 1978 *net* fuel imports into oil-importing ldcs were equal to only 4 % of total imports, against 16 % for dcs[2]). They were harder hit by inflation in the prices of their manufactured imports (which was itself partly a consequence of higher oil costs), whose prices rose by 40 % in 1973–75. With their export prices rising more slowly, there was a 12 % worsening in the ldcs terms of trade in 1974 alone, followed by a smaller deterioration in 1975.

The governments of those countries suddenly forced heavily into deficit were faced with three alternative lines of action:

- to *finance* the deficits by borrowing and running down reserves in the hope that the deficits would prove temporary;
- to *restructure*: to recognise that the deficits were not temporary and to use reserves and borrowings in order to tide over a period when the domestic economy was restructured to lessen dependence on oil and other imports, and to stimulate new exports;
- to *deflate*: to minimise both borrowing and restructuring by holding down domestic consumption and investment in order to limit the demand for imports and exportables.

The governments of those OPEC members with major surpluses also had to make important decisions – about what to do with their surpluses.[3] How best to invest their surpluses so as to earn a satisfactory return and maintain their real value, against the day when they would be needed to pay for imports? The simple geography of the global balance of payments indicated a requirement for large financial flows from the OPEC bloc to the rest of the Third World. However, it could hardly be expected that the bloc would be willing to provide more than a fraction of total surpluses as concessionary aid and, in any case, there were formidable institutional constraints on such a massive expansion in this type of flow. In the event, the OPEC countries did expand their aid about ten-fold in 1972–75 – no mean achievement – but this absorbed only a small part of the surpluses and most of the money went to a handful of non-oil Arab countries.[4] Somehow it was necessary to reconcile the surplus countries' objectives as investors with a need for further large flows to the deficit countries.

Since intermediation is a traditional role of bankers, this task of recycling was a natural one for the international banks. Nevertheless, there were many who doubted their ability to cope, because the sums involved were very large in relation to the size of the international banking system in the early 1970s. In fact, the system responded strongly and there was an enormous growth in international bank lending. The Eurocurrency market, which consists of foreign-currency lending by European banks and by subsidiaries of American and other non-European banks based in Europe, was prominent in this expansion. This can be seen from the figures of annual bank lending in Table 5.4, showing a twelve-fold increase in total lending in 1972–79. Whether this met the requirements of the global economy is an issue to which we return shortly.

Before doing so we should note the dc reaction to the 1974 oil crisis and its implications for ldcs. Taking the group as a whole, the dcs opted largely for a combination of financing and deflation. While it is true that dc energy consumption has fallen relative to GDP since 1973, most of this change has resulted from a normal demand elasticity response to higher relative energy prices rather than from government-initiated moves for economic re-structuring. Indeed, government failures to pass the full extent of oil price rises on to final users has limited restructuring through demand elasticity, and the proportion of total dc energy requirements which are met by oil is unchanged at the 1973 level.[5]

The automatically deflationary effects of higher oil prices were reinforced by policies to restrain government spending and domestic credit. This caused large losses of output and employment, with declining per capita incomes in the dcs during 1974 and 1975, while inflation

Table 5.4 *Growth of the Euromarket and its Lending to LDCs*
(Values in $ billion)

| | Euro-currency bank credit to: | | |
	All countries (1)	Non-OPEC LDCs (2)	(2) as % of (1) (3)
1972	6.8	1.5	22
1973	21.9	4.5	21
1974	29.3	6.3	22
1975	21.0	8.2	39
1976	28.8	11.0	38
1977	41.8	13.5	32
1978	70.2	26.9	38
1979	82.8	35.4	43

Source: Morgan Guaranty, *World Financial Markets* (various issues).

remained rapid. Depression in the dcs (plus a retreat into protectionist measures against manufactured goods from developing countries) meant reduced demand and lower relative prices for ldc exports; and the continuing rapid inflation meant higher prices for the manufactured goods imported by ldcs. The effect of these changes was both to protect the payments situations of the dcs and to shift much of the payments burden associated with the OPEC surpluses onto the developing countries, as is apparent from Table 5.3.[6] A less deflationary stance, giving greater emphasis to making new investments so as to adjust economic structures to the new international environment, would have bolstered world demand for ldc exports, limited the size of OPEC surpluses and thus reduced the counterpart deficits in the Third World.

Recycling and the developing countries

How, then did the (non-oil) ldcs cope with the large deficits they found themselves with and what was the role of the Eurocurrency market in this context? If we consider ldcs as a bloc, the evidence in Table 5.5 suggests that they were more than able to meet their financing needs. Some emphasis has been placed in public discussions on the fact that they were able to build up their international reserves in this period – by $39 billion according to Table 5.5 – but it would be quite wrong to infer from this that ldcs were not left with major payments problems. First, it is a mistake to regard the capital flows purely as a compensating response to a financing gap. In some degree the size of the gap is determined by the availability of finance: countries which cannot borrow what they need are forced to cut back on imports, a point to which we return. Second, most of the apparent increase in reserves is a result of money illusion. The dollar value of external reserves held by ldcs increased by 145 % in 1973–79 but in the same period the unit prices of their imports went up by 124 %. Deflated by the import price index, the real value of reserves rose only 9 % in these six years. Expressed in relation to actual imports, reserves actually diminished – from the equivalent of 5.0 months' imports at end-1973 to 3.3 months' imports at end-1979.[7] Third, the increase in the nominal value of reserves was accompanied by a much larger increase in external indebtedness, some of which should appropriately be netted out against reserves. Thus, in 1973–78, ldc non-monetary short-term debt liabilities increased by $13 billion, in addition to much more sizeable increases in medium-to-long-term indebtedness to commercial banks. Indeed, the rapid growth in ldc debt is increasingly giving concern.

Returning now to the figures in Table 5.5, these also show that in nominal (but again not real) amounts, there were large increases in the two traditional vehicles of recycling – aid (line 2) and direct investment (line 3).[8] But the really decisive change was the enormous rise in the

Table 5.5 *Current Account Financing of Non-oil LDC Deficits, 1969–78*

(US $ billions)

		1969–73	1974–78
1.	Aggregate current account deficit[a]	45	146
Financed by:			
2.	Transfers and concessionary aid loans	31	59
3.	Direct investments (net)	10	26
4.	Non-concessionary long-term loans	–[b]	24
5.	Borrowings from private financial institutions and through bond issues	8	61
6.	Use of IMF and similar facilities	0	7
7.	*less* Additions to foreign exchange reserves	–19	–39
8.	All other items, including errors and omissions (net)	15	8
9.	Total financing	45	146

Source: IMF *Annual Reports*, 1976 and 1979.

Notes: a – Excluding official transfers, which are counted as a financing item, below.

b – Included in the line 2 figure.

amount of financing available through the international banking system (line 5), increasing to a total of $61 billions in 1974–78 from only $8 billions in the previous five years. The same trend of very rapid expansion is also to be observed for the Euromarket from the second column of Table 5.4. The third column of Table 5.4 also shows the ldc share of total Eurocurrency lending to have nearly doubled in 1973–78, although almost all the increased share occurred in 1974–75.

On the basis of evidence such as this, the general view is that Euromarket and lending by other international banking centres was highly effective in meeting the financing needs of non-oil developing countries in this period.[9] There is, however, a large element of myth in this view, which has grown up on the basis of a number of confusions.

First, there has been a tendency to confuse demand with supply, and to confuse demand for commercial bank loans with payments needs. Commentators are apt to point to the increased volume of lending (supply) as evidence that the banks are meeting demand, especially for the countries with the largest deficits. Naturally, we do not hear about the size of *unsuccessful* ldc efforts to raise loans. More seriously, it seems certain in view of evidence presented shortly that many of the poorer developing countries have been deterred by high interest rates or by (probably realistic) pessimism about their credit ratings from entering the market at all, even though their need for additional foreign exchange is scarcely in doubt. Instead they have had to limit their current account deficits by deflation and by restricting imports. It is, of course, not the job of international bankers to arrange their asset portfolios so that ldcs can meet their development aspirations but it is precisely for this type of reason that calls for a new international economic order are voiced so persistently.

Second, in assessing the contribution of Eurocurrency market there has been a confusion between gross and net flows. The figures provided in Tables 5.4 and 5.5 are gross but what is much more significant is the question, what was the *net* flow to ldcs? Since non-oil ldcs are major depositors with the banks, as well as borrowers, there are large differences between the gross and net figures. This is shown by Table 5.6, from which it can be seen in the bottom line that net lending to ldcs taken as a group was well under half of the gross figure. To a substantial extent the banks have merely been re-lending ldc deposits – a useful service but not a major contribution to global recycling.

The geographical breakdown in Table 5.6 is of even greater interest, however, for it reveals the very heavy concentration of *net* lending in Latin America, and in a few countries of that region. Latin America in fact absorbed almost all the net total of Euromarket lending to non-oil

Table 5.6   *Gross and Net Euromarket Lending to Non-oil Ldcs as at end–1979[a]*

	($ billion)	
	gross	*net*
Middle East	8.2	− 7.8
Asia	33.1	6.5
Africa	14.0	4.7
Latin America	103.5	65.1
of which, the five main borrowers:[b]		
Argentina	(13.1)	(5.4)
Brazil	(36.9)	(28.8)
Liberia	(6.8)	(4.4)
Mexico	(30.7)	(22.5)
S. Korea	(10.3)	(7.2)
Sub-total, 5 countries	(97.8)	(68.3)
All non-oil ldcs	158.8	68.5

Source: Bank for International Settlements, *Annual Report*, 1979–80 and 'International banking developments-first quarter 1980' (BIS, Basle, July 1980).

Note: a − The gross figure is of total Euromarket bank claims; the net figure is of claims minus liabilities.

 b − Financial centres in ldcs excluded.

ldcs; lending to Argentina, Brazil and Mexico alone was equivalent to 83 % of the net total. Africa and Asia were net recipients on only a minor scale; the Middle East was a net depositor. In short, access to the recycling activities of the Euromarket was exceedingly unequal and geographically concentrated. The five largest net borrowers listed in Table 5.6 between them accounted for 99.7 % of the recorded net total.

As has already been implied, the criteria employed by banks to decide credit rating are quite unrelated to the tests that might be employed, say, by aid agencies to determine development needs. Although judgements about likely future political developments no doubt carry a good deal of weight, the main economic variables which provide significant statistical explanations of access to commercial bank credit are the level, variability and expected future growth of exports, the overall growth performance of the economy and the projected debt servicing-exports ratio.[10] These tests in fact favour the more advanced ldcs, so that access to credit is positively correlated with per capita income.[11]

The skewed distribution of ldc access to Euromarket lending is further demonstrated in Table 5.7. Take first the gross lending in the 'liabilities' column. What emerges from this is that ldc financial centres have been

Table 5.7 *Developing Country Assets and Liabilities with the Eurocurrency Market, as at March 1980*

Developing country grouping	Assets	($ billion) Liabilities	Net balance[a]
1. Oil exporting countries	104.2	38.4	+ 65.8
2. Financial centres[b]	126	140.2	− 14.1
3. Other developing countries	94.5	167.3	− 72.8
of which:[c]			
(a) Upper-income ldcs	60.5	119.7	− 59.2
(b) Middle-income ldcs	26.1	43.2	− 17.1
(c) Lower-income ldcs	7.9	4.4	+ 3.5
4. Grand Total	324.8	345.9	− 21.1

Source: Computed from BIS 'International banking developments' *op. cit.* and World Bank, *World Atlas, 1979.*

Notes: a − A minus sign indicates net borrowing from the Eurocurrency market; a plus indicates net deposits and other assets.

b − Bahamas, Cayman Islands, Panama, Lebanon, Hong Kong and Singapore.

c − Defined according to 1978 per capita incomes, as:
    upper income = above $1000,
    middle income = $300–1000,
    lower-income = below $300.

very large recipients of Eurocredits and that even the oil exporters have been borrowing on a large scale. Among other ldcs, the upper-income countries (those with per capita incomes of more than $1,000) have obtained the lion's share, with the middle income countries also attracting substantial amounts and the low-income countries (per capita incomes below $300) scarcely getting a look in. The 'net balance' column is even more interesting. The oil exporters of course emerge as large net depositors, while the net borrowing of the financial centres is revealed as only a tenth of their gross borrowings.[12] Among the other ldcs, the predominance of upper-income countries is even more overwhelming and *the lower-income countries are net depositors.* On an admittedly small scale, *the credit criteria of the Euromarket have in effect resulted in a transfer of funds from the poorest to the richest ldcs.* There is, no doubt, force in the defence that many of the poorest ldcs would be bad credit risks, but one should not exaggerate the sagacity of the banks' own lending policies. The fact is that these have resulted in a very heavy concentration of banking risks on a small number of ldcs, partly as a result of active loan salesmanship.[13] Such a concentration has left the international banking system highly vulnerable to political and economic conditions in a few key, persistent deficit, ldcs. This does not offer a viable lending policy in the longer term, especially in a world of high interest rates. Continued heavy lending to the favoured few results in mounting debt servicing burdens, so that even by 1978 (latest data available) the cost of debt interest and repayment of the 'big two' borrowers relative to their export earnings was 28% and 60% for Brazil and Mexico respectively.[14] Easy access to large loans from banks only too anxious to lend may also permit governments to defer unpopular measures needed to strengthen their economies. In the longer term both factors will weaken the borrowers' credit ratings.

But whatever view we take of the lending policies of the Eurobanks and however useful the Euromarket may be as a vehicle for the profitable investment of ldc foreign exchange reserves, we are bound to conclude from the evidence in Table 5.7 that international monetary arrangements have singularly failed to meet the financing needs of lower-income ldcs. This must modify the received opinion that international banking was instrumental in allowing ldcs to cover their payments deficits in the 1974–78 period. In fact, it was only a fortunate and relatively prosperous minority which had major access to the banks, because of which they were able to expand imports and run large current deficits. At least some of the countries in this category are 'developing countries' by convention only. The economic characteristics of Mexico and Brazil have a good deal more in common with dcs than with the economies of Africa, Asia and much of the rest of the Western Hemisphere. The majority of 'genuine' ldcs were confronted by a far more severe foreign exchange constraint. Indeed, after 1973 the lower-income ldcs had to cut sharply back on imports. And, while there is no automatic link between import capacity and economic growth, which is influenced by numerous other factors, it is unlikely to be a coincidence that output has grown fastest in the countries with the more rapidly expanding import volumes (% growth rates in 1970–78):[15]

	GDP	import volume
low-income ldcs	3.6	3.2
middle- and upper-income ldcs	5.7	5.8

1979 and beyond: the re-emergence of major disequilibria

After a 13% decline, relative to the prices of industrial exports, in 1977–78, there was a further major rise in the real price of oil in 1979–80. Starting from a little under $13 per barrel at the beginning of 1979, the average price of crude was up to $31 by May 1980–a 138% increase in a year and a half. In the same period the volume of imports by the OPEC bloc failed to show as rapid an expansion as had characterised 1974–78 (when it grew at 24% p.a.) and there were doubts about the future capacity of this group of countries to increase their import absorption at the rate of those earlier years. In consequence, having seen the pattern of international payments revert in 1978 to what appeared to be pre-1974 normality (see Table 5.3), the world was once again faced with major disequilibria in the global balance of payments. This can be observed in the right-hand column of Table 5.3. The figures are only approximate estimates but there is no doubt about the basic trends they reveal: huge surpluses by the oil exporting group, and large deteriorations in the current accounts of both industrial and non-oil developing countries. The international monetary system now has the task of recycling even larger surpluses from OPEC to the deficit areas.

Opinions are divided about the most probable course of events after 1980.[16] The large oil price increases of 1979–80 and the depression in the industrial world must slacken the demand for oil and inhibit the power of oil exporters to achieve further large real price increases (although these factors did not prevent another increase in May 1980, partly because the oil consuming nations have so far achieved limited reduction in their dependence on oil imports). The volume of OPEC imports is likely to resume an upward trend, if a less steep one than formerly. The OPEC surplus, while remaining very large in 1981, can therefore be expected to diminish thereafter. The probability nevertheless remains that the banks will continue to receive large net OPEC deposits during the next few years and that the recycling task will remain a major one.

The way in which the dcs react to the deterioration in their current accounts will exert a powerful influence on the course of events. Were they to repeat their deflationary policies of 1974–75, the effect would be to shift a large additional portion of the counter-part deficits of the OPEC surpluses onto the ldcs. This would make it unlikely that the banks alone could undertake the recycling task, given their traditional lending policies, and would likely have seriously damaging effects on the prospects for poverty alleviation in the lower-income ldcs. The industrial world is already in a depression, of course, although a less severe one than that of 1974–75. The growth of investment remains sluggish and most dc governments are still applying restrictive fiscal and monetary policies in pursuit of reduced inflation. These factors, and the continuing absence of strong action to reduce oil import dependence through restructuring, bode ill for the developing world.

The real price of non-oil ldc exports is already far below its 1973–74 peak but they too have higher import bills to pay (a $1 increase in the price of a barrel of oil imposes an aggregate balance of payments cost on non-oil ldcs of $2 billions – and the price went up by $18 in the 17 months from the beginning of 1979).[17] Ldcs can also expect continuing inflation and higher energy costs in the dcs to further boost the prices of industrial imports. Depression in the dcs will also hit demand for ldc exports, with OECD estimating that every percentage point reduction in dc growth reduces ldc export earnings by $2 billions.[18] So developing countries' terms of trade are worsening once again and their current deficits – already exceptionally large in 1979 – are expected to plunge to new record levels in 1980 and 1981. It is true that as a group, they have a larger cushion of foreign exchange reserves to fall back on than was the case in 1974, but we have already shown the real value of this increase is modest and that the cushion is now thinner in terms of months of imports. It is also significant that the IMF has recently felt impelled to express its 'utmost concern' about the increasing number of ldcs falling into arrears in payments for imports and other foreign exchange obligations.[19]

Overall, then, the development prospects of ldcs have been put severely at risk by current global trends. That they stand to be more seriously affected by present imbalances than they were in 1974–75 is now generally acknowledged: by OECD, the IMF, the World Bank, and even by the June 1980 Venice summit of Western heads of government. It is against this background that we must view the prospects for financial flows and for Euromarket recycling.

Recycling in the 1980s

As is apparent from the foregoing, the logic of the global balance of payments is that massive financial flows are required from the OPEC surplus countries to the rest of the Third World and to the dcs. This naturally focuses attention on the issue of development aid from oil producers.[20] After a dramatic rise in the first half of the 1970s, the real value of disbursed OPEC aid peaked in 1975 and by 1978 was barely half the 1975 level. As in the mid-seventies, the OPEC bloc again has the financial resources for major increases and this time it has more of an institutional base from which to launch a major new effort. But the motivations are no longer as strong as they were in the seventies and, notwithstanding protestations of solidarity with the remainder of the Third World, it seems unlikely that enlarged OPEC aid flows will make a major contribution to ldc recycling needs.

That the dcs will receive a massive infusion of capital from OPEC is not, however, in doubt; only the financial centres of the West can handle the enormous sums involved. Thus, one further possibility is that OPEC surpluses might be 're-recycled' to ldcs in the form of enlarged aid flows from the West. Again, it is difficult to be sanguine. The real value of Western aid has been static, even declining, in recent years (note 8) and, in relation to GNP, is only half the UN target level. Neither in the USA nor in Europe is there a political impetus for substantially enlarged aid flows, and the bold initiatives proposed by the Brandt Report have been received there with less than acclaim.

In short, while ldcs have a massively increased financing requirement the aid lobby will probably feel it has done well if it manages to maintain the real value of existing levels. The large residual financing requirement will have to be met – if it is met at all – by the banks, which brings us back to the Eurocurrency market. Here too grounds for optimism are hard to find. Commercial banks have, in fact, become concerned about their exposure levels in developing countries, for a number of reasons. We have already shown that the heavy concentration of bank lending on Brazil, Mexico and a few other ldcs has left the banks with a rather risky portfolio of overseas claims in countries which have experienced rapidly rising debt servicing obligations, and the profitability of international lending has been low relative to this risk. Political turmoil, a payments crisis and debt repudiation in one of the big borrowers could thus have the gravest consequences for world banking. The rapid expansion of international lending has led to what are regarded as deteriorating ratios both of international to domestic lending, and of loans to capital. Jogged, perhaps, by the reverberations of President Carter's freezing of Iranian bank deposits, the central bank governors of the major industrial countries agreed in April 1980 on measures that would permit stricter monitoring and supervision of international banking developments and reaffirmed 'the cardinal importance which they attach to the maintenance of sound banking standards . . . '[21] Significantly, there was no reference whatever in the text of their statement to the financing needs of ldcs.

With commercial bankers themselves expressing concern at their degree of exposure, with world interest rates still at high levels and with monetary authorities moving towards a stricter supervision of international lending, the Euromarket is now expanding much more slowly – at 15–20% p.a. in current prices, compared with nearly 40% p.a. in 1972–78. Indeed, lending to ldcs in the first half of 1980 was little more than half the figure for the same part of 1979.[22] The banks were showing diminished enthusiasm for large new OPEC deposits. There was hence a deceleration precisely during a period of accelerating needs (although this was thought to be due partly to negotiating tactics by the traditionally large ldc borrowers).

If these factors are considered alongside our earlier demonstration that Euromarket lending did nothing for the financing needs of the hard core, low-income ldcs even in the period of rapid expansion, it is easy to conclude that the commercial banks, by themselves and within the traditions of 'sound banking standards', will not meet the large residual financing requirements of most poorer ldcs. Perhaps in recognition of this, the World Bank has introduced a new 'structural adjustment' loan facility but the Bank is short of funds and lending from this facility will be at less than $1 billion a year. There have also been moves for the International Monetary Fund to play an increased role, by borrowing from the OPEC surplus countries and re-lending to deficit ldcs. But the fact is that even some of the Fund's existing facilities are under-utilised and are likely to remain so until there is some relaxation in the stringent policy conditions which are often attached to them. Substantial loosening of the policy strings would be necessary for a major expansion of the Fund's role but there is no sign that the dc government representatives who dominate the Fund's boards are yet in a mood to permit such softening. Repetition of the OPEC-financed oil facilities set up in 1974 and 1975 also seems unlikely.

Thus, we arrive at a gloomy conclusion. In the absence of a means for reconciling development needs with the requirements of banking prudence, the Euromarket, and international banking generally, will not supply the import financing capacity that would be needed if the 'hard core' ldcs were to maintain even moderate economic progress. For reasons such as these the World Bank has warned for 1980–85 of a danger of declining per capita incomes in Africa and of increased numbers of people living in absolute poverty. Even the more prosperous ldcs are expected to suffer serious declines in the expansion rate of average incomes.[23]

With most ldcs substantially excluded from recycling flows, there will probably be an excess of OPEC surpluses over the financing demands of the industrial world. Banks will become less enthusiastic about accepting OPEC deposits and an excess supply of funds will tend to depress Euromarket interest rates (and hence the rates of return received by OPEC members from their oil surpluses). While the OPEC surplus countries can buy non-financial assets in the West, such as investments in industry and property, there will be limits to their ability and willingness to do so.[24] It may thus be borne in on the governments of the OPEC surplus countries that oil in the ground is their best investment for the future and that the best strategy is to reduce (or fail to expand) production.

The prospect of a major depression in ldcs, and perhaps of a sellers' market for oil, cannot be good news for the industrial West either. Ldc stagnation would make it all the harder for the West to recover from its own depression; so would yet higher real oil prices. Severe strains within the international banking system could also spell dangers for the West. But perhaps it needs a major banking disturbance to jolt political leaderships into reforms that would better meet the recycling needs of the global economy.

The EEC and Energy Aid to the Third World

Kurt Hoffman and David Burch

Introduction

In recent years concern has been expressed at the highest levels about present and future patterns of energy supply and demand. World energy consumption in 1975 was about 5,750 million t. o. e (tonnes of oil equivalent) and in the year 2000 it is estimated that it will be between 15,000 million and 20,000 million t. o. e. At a global level, per capita energy consumption in 1975 was 1.45 t. o. e but there were significant differences between the developed and underdeveloped countries. In 1975 per capita consumption of commercial energy in USA was 7.8 t. o. e and in Europe it was 3.1 t. o. e; yet in the developing countries the level of per capita consumption was only 0.3 t. o. e. Put more simply, about 30 % of the world's population (located in the developed countries) consume about 83 % of the available energy (Commission of the European Communities (CEC) 1978).

Despite these significant differences, it has been suggested that the energy crisis is nevertheless a problem affecting the developed and underdeveloped countries alike. This is said to be especially true where oil is concerned; for example, the European Community has pointed out that whilst in 1975 (before North Sea oil) it imported some 57 % of its oil requirements, the ACP states associated with the Community under the Lomé Conventions import over 80 % of their commercial energy requirements, while only a few ACP states are major energy producers (oil in Nigeria, Gabon, Congo and Trinidad and Tobago; uranium in Niger and Gabon).

In an era characterised by rising prices for increasingly scarce supplies of oil, continuing dependence of both the EEC and the ACP states on imported oil could lead to damaging competition that should be avoided if possible. Moreover, various studies forecasting future trends in energy consumption suggest that the existing inequalities cited above will continue well into the 21st century, raising the possibility of increasing rather than lessening tensions between the two groups (CEC, 1978; Cheshire and Pavitt, 1978). Given this situation, the European Community has argued that energy provides an increasingly important area not of confrontation but for mutual co-operation with the ACP states through means of the Community's aid programmes. It is felt that such collaboration could benefit the developing countries by assisting them to increase their levels of energy consumption and conversion efficiency; while at the same time helping them to develop new sources of energy which would thereby relieve some of the financial burden imposed by energy imports. (Europe Information, 1979). Equally important, EEC countries would themselves benefit from the increased ACP demand for their goods and services which would result directly from the aid programmes and more generally from the improved living conditions in the Third World brought about by better access to energy. This sort of return to investments in aid has been deemed very important, by EEC spokesmen, as making a potentially major contribution to the momentum of the Community's economic recovery in the 1980's.

Aid for Energy

As a result of this recognition of mutual interests in energy aid, the European Community finances numerous aid projects in the energy sector of the ACP states. The sources of finance for this are several, including the European Investment Bank (EIB), the European Development Fund (EDF), and the national aid programmes of member states. Total aid for energy co-operation in the underdeveloped countries, provided both by member states and the European Community as a whole in 1979 amounted to Eua 500 million ($680 million). In 1980, this total is expected to exceed Eua 800 million. Setting national programmes aside, EEC aid for energy co-operation under the first Lomé Convention amounted to Eua 190 million ($260 million) by November 1979, with Eua 113 million coming from the European Development Fund and Eua 77 million from the European Investment Bank. In turn, this direct contribution, supported by co-financing arrangements, has allowed investments valued at about Eua 910 million ($1,250 million) to be undertaken (CEC, 1978). The Community contribution was allocated to projects concerned with hydroelectric power, thermal energy, power transmission and alternative energy sources.

A detailed breakdown of these projects is provided at the end of this section. It shows that investments in hydroelectric projects account for the greatest proportion of funds, around 74%, while thermal energy production and transmission together form the second largest category of projects and takes up about 19 % of total aid for energy co-operation. Most of these projects are being undertaken in the African states. The primary emphasis on hydro power is partly a reflection of the conventional pattern of funding adopted by other major international agencies such as the World Bank. It can also be seen as a response to the drought in the Sahel region, where the construction of dams is thought to be the only means of stabilising a rapidly deteriorating situation. This bias towards hydropower is broadly in line with the existence of considerable hydropower potential in developing countries in general and in Africa in particular, which accounts for some 40 % of total world potential (Hilling, 1976). One of the characteristics of this potential is that much of it is concentrated in relatively small streams and rivers not suitable for the large scale projects traditionally financed by aid flows. Mini and micro hydro technology is necessary to exploit this potential but unfortunately this is not an area where adequate levels of aid are being directed at the moment. It is conceivable that the EEC could make its hydropower aid programme more effective by re-orienting part of it towards smaller scale projects at the community level.

The smallest category of aid flow relates to projects concerned with alternative energy sources; these account for only about 7 % of the total. This category of projects is significant not because of its size (although it is expected that aid to this area will grow rapidly) but because the Community feels that alternative energy sources are likely to be highly appropriate to the needs of the majority of the developing countries. (Europe Information, 1979). Currently, two large-scale projects account for Eua 9 million of the Eua 13 million devoted to alternative energy sources; a project for geothermal energy production in Ethiopia at Eua 4.1 million, and a thermal power station with wood gasification in Guyana at Eua 5 million. Most of the remaining investment is in solar energy. This area of activity accounted for 9 projects totalling Eua 2.3 million at the end of 1978, and increased to 13 projects accounting for Eua 3.035 million by the end of 1979.

Future Energy Aid

The EEC is proposing to make a significant increase in aid for energy co-operation with developing countries. This is confirmed by the greater emphasis given to energy in Lomé II. The first Lomé Convention made only passing references to aid in the energy sector; when discussing industrial, technical and financial co-operation and when outlining certain financial arrangements touching upon oil exploration. However, Lomé II makes specific provision in Article 76 (reproduced in the documentary appendix) for aid to the energy sector. It discusses the means (investment, technology transfer, training, research, exploration, compilation of inventories and other studies) by which the associated states can achieve the aim of self-sufficiency in energy. Finance for oil exploration will continue on only a modest scale, since resources are not available for aid in this sector under Lomé II. But the Community has indicated that more aid will be available to exploit energy resources in the form of:

(a) Traditional, but as yet unexploited resources such as coal, peat and hydroelectric power.
(b) New sources, such as solar, wind and geothermal, biomass, methane gas etc.

While conventional energy sources will probably continue to dominate future policy in this area, the Community programme (though as yet unclear in its specific details of allocations to various sectors) does seem to suggest a shift in emphasis towards alternative and renewable energy resources. Among the range of renewable energy sources, solar energy seems to have been picked out as a significant area for future co-operation. Certainly, the Community seems to be encouraging this, and prior to the final agreement on Lomé II, the Commission stated that it would like to see reference in the new Convention to a greater number of 'microprojects' (solar pumps, solar furnaces and solar televisions). Other Community documents have dealt with the issue of solar energy and development, pointing to achievements and prospects in this area corresponding to precise needs under Lomé II. This emphasis probably reflects the Community's interest in the development of solar technology for use within member countries. A number of solar energy projects comprise a major item in the 1980–83 Joint Research Centre's (JRC) Multiannual Research Programme,[25] and this solar energy programme has provision for technical assistance to the underdeveloped countries (Europe Information, 1979).

In the above discussion we have tried to demonstrate that the EEC has recognised the importance of providing energy aid to the developing countries and has committed itself to funding a growing number of activities in this area. We have noted that the orientation of its aid in the commercial energy sector towards hydropower is generally correct and that in attaching importance to the provision of technical assistance in exploiting alternative energy sources the Community is drawing upon its own growing body of expertise in this area as well as reflecting a wider view that these sources have much future potential (Hayes, 1977).

A priori, these aid efforts are encouraging since the developing countries do have a considerable need for some form of assistance with their energy problems. However, the Community has also emphasised that it is concerned to ensure that its aid efforts do actually meet the real needs of the developing countries and lead to an improvement in living standards. Given this concern, there are grounds for asking if the Community's aid efforts are being channelled in *the most effective manner* to meet its objectives of assisting the developing countries to improve their living standards. This question is particularly important in the light of the Community's equally important objective of promoting the export of energy technology from its member states to the Third World. Of course, this is a perfectly acceptable concern on the part of the EEC. However the possibility does arise that there could be a conflict of interest between the (already well-documented) export activities of private sector solar energy firms motivated by a search for profits and the social concerns of the Community to assist the Third World. (See Agarwal, 1978; Hoffman, 1980; UNCTAD, 1978.)

Obviously a proper evaluation of the relative costs and benefits of the Community's energy aid efforts can only be done on a project by project basis which also takes into account the net effect of private sector activities in this area. Unfortunately we are not in a position to do this at this time although we do recommend that such evaluations be systematically carried out in the future by both the Community and independent observers. Nevertheless, a good deal of information does exist on the nature of the Third World energy problems, on the orientation of Community aid efforts and on the ongoing private sector initiatives of member states. A brief review of this literature would allow us to at least raise some questions about the general direction of EEC activities and suggest some criteria that might usefully be taken into consideration during a more comprehensive assessment.

Energy in the Third World

In assessing the relevance and value of the Community's programme of energy aid to ACP countries, it seems a good idea to start by considering its view of the nature of the energy problems facing developing countries. A review of Community statements shows that the EEC is mostly concerned about Third World problems associated with low levels of consumption of the commercial forms of energy such as oil, coal, and indirectly, electricity (CEC, 1979; Europe Information, 1979). The Community, of course, is not alone in the view that per capita consumption of commercial energy must rise in developing countries in order for the average levels of income to rise. This perception of the problem is perhaps partly responsible for the fact that 60–80 % (much of it partially aid funded) of all public sector energy investments in developing countries are usually aimed at increasing centralised electric power capacity (Hayes, 1977; World Bank, 1975). On balance, the Community appears to be much less concerned about the problems associated with the use of non-commercial traditional fuels such as wood fuel, animal dung and crop residues. These aspects of Third World energy consumption are given relatively little consideration (and aid funds). The Community's primary concerns in this area are focussed on the environmental problems, such as deforestation, which it feels are caused by the high demand for firewood.

This perception of the energy problem (although common) un-fortunately does not adequately reflect the situation which is in fact portrayed in the rapidly burgeoning literature related to Third World energy problems. It is becoming increasingly apparent that traditional energy sources account for a very large majority of total energy consumed in many Third World countries. These fuels are certainly the dominant energy source in the rural areas of most African and Asian countries (Earl, 1975; French, 1978) For instance, fuelwood, consumed either as charcoal or firewood, contributes 96% of all energy consumed in Tanzania, 91% in Nigeria and 90% in Uganda (Eckholm, 1975). Many observers feel that this extensive dependence on traditional fuels, particularly firewood, is the major energy problem Third World countries are likely to face over the next 10 years. The Community is making an important mistake in its assumption that the ACP states depend heavily for their energy requirements on imported oil. This fact relates only to commercial forms of energy; when non-commercial energy forms are included then the picture changes dramatically.[26] Commercial energy sources really account for only a relatively small percentage of total energy consumed; although this percentage is likely to be higher in some of the Latin American and Caribbean states. Correspondingly, commer-cial energy meets the energy needs of only a small fraction of the population in developing countries. Demand for commercial energy is highly concentrated in the urban areas, particularly in the transportation (largely private cars) and industrial sectors. Urban areas typically contain only a relatively small percentage of the total population – but this percentage usually accounts for the overwhelming majority of upper income groups in the country. In Africa, for example, only 10% of the population, usually the wealthiest 10%, lives in urban areas, and they consume 95% of all commercial fuels used in the country (OECD, 1979).

This means that most of the Community's energy projects related to conventional energy (about 93% of all energy aid) would appear to be directed at only a relatively small, well-off proportion of the population. It is unlikely that many rural people will benefit from these investments in centralised energy supply projects since only about 12% of all rural areas in developing countries have access to electricity. There is, however, some variation between continents, with access open to 23% of rural areas in Latin America, 15% in Asia, 15% in the Middle East and only 4% in Southern Asia. Many observers feel that this coverage will only be extended slowly in the wealthier developing countries and not at all among the poorer countries (Hayes, 1977).

In addition there appear to be serious problems of technology dependency associated with commercial (or conventional) energy aid projects. Some studies have shown that Third World countries are excessively dependent upon conventional energy systems imported from the advanced industrial countries such as electricity production and transmission equipment. Moreover, due to the monopolistic position of the developed country technology suppliers, developing countries are often required to pay unnecessarily high prices for their equipment which are well above the market prices paid by developed countries (Epstein and Mirow, 1977; Newfarmer, 1978). Frequently, financial support and technical assistance for commercial energy projects, (which is rarely adequate to meet more than a small share of total costs) is provided by national and international donors in the form of tied aid which tends to force aid recipients to acquire foreign technology in the first instance. This in turn often leads to continued reliance on foreign sources of supply. Consequently, this long term dependence on imported technology not only has financial costs but also means that developing countries may be denied the opportunity of developing a local technological capacity in a crucial sector. (See Hoffman, 1980 and UNCTAD, 1978 for a more extensive discussion.) From the available evidence, it is not possible to say if the EEC conventional energy aid projects to the ACP states have had similar effects to those described above, although the amounts of aid that have been provided by the Community are substantial. Analysis to assess the net benefit of the projects must take into account the elements of social and financial cost outlined above. We would suggest that such an evaluation be given the highest priority by the Community.

If we turn our attention to the Community's efforts in the area of alternative energy, a different set of concerns arise. The Community appears to be concentrating its attention on solar energy projects with only a small amount of effort as yet being devoted to other sources such as biomass and wind power. This bias may be the result of the Community's view that solar energy systems are ideally suited to meet the energy needs of rural people. To support their work in this field, the Commission held a symposium at Varese, Italy in March 1979, on 'Solar Energy in the Service of the Developing Countries'. The purpose of the symposium was 'to define the needs of the developing countries in this field and to look for methods of rationalising research activities and efforts in this area'. However, as we have argued earlier this orientation also possibly stems from the importance that the Community attaches to developing an indigenous solar energy industry among its member states.

Whatever the reason, this focus on alternative energy systems, particularly the solar energy aspect, merits a number of observations. Firstly, it is not yet clear that solar energy systems are the most suitable systems. It is true that they have a number of technical characteristics which may be suitable in rural areas; but then so do many other systems. Unfortunately, there have been few attempts to carry out field-based economic, social and technical evaluations of *competing* alternative energy technologies. The more usual situation discussed in the literature is one where pilot projects are evaluated either individually or else are compared against other systems on the basis of data drawn from laboratory or theoretical conditions (Barnett et al., 1978). Such evaluations are clearly an inadequate basis on which to decide the allocation of resources to investment in solar energy systems or any other technical alternatives. The Community should review the grounds on which it is attaching so much importance to solar energy as the solution to rural energy systems. Clearly any sizeable investment in the production and distribution of solar energy systems should only be done after full evaluations have been carried out.

Secondly, as one of the Community documents points out, there may be considerable difficulties in introducing alternative energy systems into rural communities. Indeed, suitability to user needs is perhaps the main factor in determining the success of the introduction of any technical system. User needs for energy conversion systems are likely to be highly location-specific and very precise. Consequently, there must be serious doubts about the extent to which systems designed in isolation from rural communities can adequately incorporate user needs and thus ensure widespread acceptance. To avoid problems of inappropriateness there must be more interaction between technologists and rural communities than the Community suggests is necessary. The Community argues for 'the importance of educating and informing the public, particularly in rural areas, before introducing solar equipment', but the technical systems are still obviously intended to be designed and produced well outside the village (CEC Spokesman Group, 1979, p.9). The extensive evidence from other sectors where a similar 'top-down' approach to introduction of new technologies was adopted, is that such efforts have little chance of widespread success (Agarwal, 1980; Dasgupta, 1977; Griffin, 1974).

Thirdly, an important aspect of 'user needs' is their ability to pay for the new systems. There is a widespread assumption in the field that low levels of energy consumption in the rural areas are due to inadequate supplies of energy (for instance due to deforestation). The policy response by many aid agencies and national governments to this perception of the problem has been one which concentrates on increasing the *supply* of energy. This has been effected largely by introducing (or proposing) new technical systems designed either to improve the conversion efficiency of currently used fuels such as wood, or to open up previously untapped sources of renewable energy such as solar power or biomass (Howe *et al.*, 1977; Usmani, 1978; Ramakumar, 1977). In fact, rather than being a problem of inadequate supply, it is more likely that low incomes prevent many of the rural poor from acquiring sufficient energy for domestic or production purposes. Income distribution is highly skewed in rural areas with much of the population existing on incomes which are close to subsistence. Lack of income is in turn related to little or no land ownership, inadequate access to credit and extension services, and low levels of technological sophistication. Any rural development programme which does not take explicit account of the distorting nature of these structural problems bears little chance of bringing benefits to those who need it most. The implication of this situation is that many technical interventions such as the introduction of solar energy systems will only benefit the wealthier fraction of the rural population who can afford the costs involved or who do not have more urgent uses for their money incomes. Once again, we cannot fully evaluate the distributional implications of the Community's ongoing alternative energy projects, but the available evidence on the *approach* being taken suggests that there may well be negative socio-economic impacts which go beyond any improvements in energy consumption which may occur.

Finally, the potential conflict between private sector interests and the Community's desire to assist Third World efforts to exploit renewable energy sources arises again. To its credit, the EEC does argue in some of its publications that it is concerned to encourage the local fabrication and production of alternative energy systems. We fully support the view that local equipment production should be encouraged wherever it is technically and economically viable even though there may be high short-run costs (Cooper and Maxwell, 1975). The problem the Community faces in advocating such a strategy is that a number of member governments, France and Germany in particular, are actively collaborating with their domestic firms to market alternative energy systems in Third World countries (Hoffman, 1980; Agarwal, 1978; UNCTAD, 1978). This problem is recognised:

> Although the ACP countries offer a fertile market on which (solar energy) equipment manufacturers already have an eye, the Commission is not going to add to the scramble for contracts (Europe Information, 1979, p.10).

The efforts of private sector firms to exploit commercial opportunities in developing countries pose a serious and potentially costly threat to the establishment of a local production capability in alternative energy systems in ACP countries as well as possibly impeding the success of any Community aid efforts in this area. Perhaps the most valuable contribution that the EEC could make (in addition to its own projects) would be to ensure that ACP countries are properly equipped to deal with the pressures to purchase what could be unnecessarily expensive and highly inappropriate technical systems from suppliers located in their member states.

EEC Energy Projects

Countries	Projects	EDF contribution '000 EUA	EIB contribution '000 EUA	Total cost '000 EUA
1 – Hydroelectric power				
Burundi Rwanda Zaïre	Ruzizi dam (study)	1.200	–	1.200
Ghana	Kpong dam	8.980	10.000	213.100
Kenya	Upper Tana dam	26.340	12.000	115.600
Malawi	Nkula Falls II dam	8.500	–	65.200
Mali	Sélingué dam	19.157	–	125.200
Sierra Leone Liberia	Mano River dam (study)	2.370	–	2.370
Rwanda	Mukungwa dam	20.000	–	30.700
Western Samoa	Magiagi dam	2.620	–	3.243
Niger	Kandadji dam (study)	1.923	–	1.923
Cameroon	Songloulou dam	–	13.500	193.830
Fiji	Hydroelectric dam	–	12.500	72.840
	Total	91.090	48.000	
		139.090		825.206
			74%	
2 – Thermal energy				
Zaïre	Butuhé power station	1.655	–	1.655
Burundi	Rural electrification	1.050	–	1.575
Upper Volta	Electrification of secondary centres	1.050	–	2.100
Guyana	Upper Demerara power station[a]	5.000	–	5.000
Mauritius	Thermal power station	–	2.000	7.120
Liberia	Bushrod power station	–	4.900	24.000
	Total	8.755	6.900	
		15.655		41.450
			8%	

a – Thermal power station with wood gasification.

EEC Energy Projects

Countries	Projects	EDF contribution '000 EUA	EIB contribution '000 EUA	Total cost '000 EUA
3 – Transmission networks				
Gape Verde	Distribution network	350	–	350
Rwanda	Kigoma–Mururu high tension line	3.900	–	3.900
Ivory Coast	Distribution network	–	11.000	11.000
Ivory Coast/ Ghana	Interconnection of networks	–	11.000	11.000
	Total	4.250	22.000	26.250
			26.250	
			14 %	
4 – Alternative energy sources				
Ethiopia	Geothermal	4.100	–	7.000
Niger	2 Solar pumps (5 and 10 KW)	550	–	550
Niger	2 KW solar motor	550	–	550
Niger	Solar water heater	5	–	5
Mauritania	Solar pump (10 KW)	475	–	475
Togo	2 Solar pumps (0.9 KW)	80	–	80
Cameroon	Solar pump (5 KW)	350	–	350
Comoros	Supply of microwave relay	200	–	200
Malawi	Solar heating of sanitary water for hospital	100	–	100
Barbados	Laboratory air conditioning (study)	25	–	25
Upper Volta	Utilization of molasses (study)	100	–	100
Sudan	Utilization of molasses (study)	115	–	115
	Total	6.650	–	9.550
			6.650	
			4 %	
	Grand Total	110.745	76.900	902.456
			187.645	
			100 %	

Taken from CEC, (1978)

Notes

1   Errors, omissions and asymmetries prevent the statistics on the world balance of payments from achieving the accountant's logic of summing to zero. Also, the figures in Table 5.3 are not complete because they exclude non-members of the IMF (including most centrally planned countries). Nevertheless, the general proposition that a surplus in one part of the system must logically have a counterpart deficit elsewhere remains valid.

2   GATT, *International Trade, 1978/79*, Table 9 (Geneva, 1979).

3   Although it is convenient for the sake of brevity to treat the oil exporting countries as a group, it should be remembered that by no means all of them have large payments surpluses. Algeria, Indonesia, Nigeria and Venezuela are among the oil exporting nations which have been net borrowers in recent years. A large part of the 'OPEC surplus' is, in fact, concentrated in Kuwait, Qatar, Saudi Arabia and the United Arab Emirates.

4   See 'OPEC aid', *ODI Briefing Paper No. 4 1980* (London, Overseas Development Institute), for an examination of these questions.

5   OECD data show that while in 1973–79 the real price of imported crude oil went up by 154 % for the seven major industrial countries, the real final price of gasoline was increased by much smaller proportions and the real final price for all forms of household energy rose by only 22 %. They also show that, measured in physical terms, oil in 1978 constituted 52.0 % of all OECD energy supplies, against 52.9 % in 1973. OECD, *Economic Outlook*, July 1980, pp. 114–130.

6   The impact of the 1973–75 industrial-country slump on ldcs is examined in more detail in 'The slump of 1980 and the Third World', *ODI Briefing Paper No. 3 1980* (London, Overseas Development Institute, April 1980).

7   These calculations are based on data in *International Financial Statistics* (various issues).

8   The proportionate increase in aid flows recorded in line 2 of Table 5.5 was almost exactly the same as the increase in import prices. Per capita aid actually fell in real terms in 1974–78.

9   cf M. S. Wionczek, 'Ldc external debt and the Euromarkets: the impressive record and the uncertain future', *World Development*, 7(2), (Oxford) February 1979.

10 See J. Eaton and M. Gersovitz, 'Ldc participation in international financial markets'. *Journal of Development Economics*, 7(1), March 1980; and I. Kapur, 'An analysis of the supply of Euro-currency finance to developing countries'. *Oxford Bulletin of Economics and Statistics*, 39(3), August 1977.

11 Eaton and Gersovitz, *op. cit.*

12 Much of the net borrowing of $14.1 bn. by the financial centres was presumably on-lent to ldc borrowers, but there is no reason to think that the distribution of this borrowing would differ strongly from the pattern revealed in items 1 and 3 of Table 5.7.

13 See OECD, 'Access of developing countries to international financial markets'. *Financial Market Trends*, No. 13, February 1980. This is critical of 'over-zealous eagerness with banks to expand lending to these countries in relation to absorptive capacity of these countries and their long-term interests'.

14   World Bank, *World Development Report, 1980* (Washington, August 1980), Annex Table 13.
15   *Ibid*, Annex Tables 2 and 8. Oil exporting countries excluded from the above.
16   See Morgan Garanty, *World Financial Markets*, March 1980 for a valuable discussion of this topic. See also OECD, *Economic Outlook*, July 1980.
17   The estimate of a $2 billion cost is from *The Economist*, 22 March 1980.
18   See OECD, *Economic Outlook*, December 1979.
19   IMF *Annual Report on Exchange Arrangements and Exchange Restrictions, 1980* (Washington, August 1980).
20   See ODI, 'OPEC aid' *op. cit.* for a fuller discussion.
21   See IMF *Survey*, 21 April 1980, pp. 113, 118.
22   See Morgan Garanty, *World Financial Markets*, June 1980.
23   World Bank, *World Development Report, 1980*, Chapt. 2. This presents alternative low and high projections of the growth of per capita incomes in the 1980s, showing, in the low case, a decline in per capita incomes in sub-Saharan Africa of 0.3 % p.a. in 1980–85 and an increase at 1.0 % for all low-income ldcs taken together. This latter rate only rises to 1.7 % in the high projection, with incomes in Africa growing at only 0.1 % p. a.
24   Some indication of past policies is given by the following estimates of the distribution of OPEC investments as at end-1978 ($ bn):

–	Financial investments in the international markets	60
–	Financial and direct investments in the U. S.	42
–	Financial and direct investments in other industrial countries	32
–	Loans and aid to Third World countries	18
–	Others (including Eastern bloc)	4
–	Financial contributions to international development institutions	12
		168

From H. S. Nashashibi in OPEC *Bulletin*, January 1980.
25   The JRC comprises four different research establishments in Belgium, Italy, the FRG and the Netherlands. It carries out the Community's own research and undertakes projects which are often beyond the scope of the member states.
26   Desai (1978) shows that by combining commercial and non commercial energy forms, including human and animal inputs in the agricultural sector, that per capita energy consumption in India is as high as in the EEC states. The important difference lies in the productivity of energy inputs, with the mechanised uses of energy yielding a much higher rate of labour productivity than the labour intensive use of energy in the Third World.

Bibliography

Agarwal, Anil., (1978), 'Solar Energy and the Third World', *New Scientist*, 9th February, 1978, pp. 357–359.

Agarwal, Bina, (1980), 'Socio-Economic Factors Affecting the Diffusion and Impact of Rural Woodfuel Technologies in the Third World', (tentative title). Mimeo. Science Policy Research Unit, University of Sussex.

Barnett, A., Pyle, L., Subramanian, S. K., (1978), *Biogas Technology in the Third World: A Multidisciplinary Review*, IDRC, Ottawa.

Chesshire, J., and Pavitt, K. (1978), 'Some Energy Futures' in *World Futures: The Great Debate* (1978), edited by Christopher Freeman and Marie Jahoda, Science Policy Research Unit, University of Sussex. Martin Robertson, London.

Commission of the European Communities, (1978), 'Energy Co-operation – Working Paper of the Services of the Commission', Brussels, December 1978.

Commission of the European Communities (1979), 'Speaking Note: Energy' Directorate-General for Development, Brussels, November 1979.

Cooper, C. M. and Maxwell, P. I. (1975), *Machinery Suppliers and the Transfer of Technology to Latin America*, Science Policy Research Unit, mimeo., University of Sussex.

Dasgupta, Biplab (1977), *Agrarian Change and the New Technology in India*, UNRISD, Geneva.

Desai, A. V., (1978), 'Development and Energy Consumption', *Oxford Bulletin of Economics and Statistics*, Vol. 40, No. 3.

Earl, D. E., (1975), *Forest Energy and Economic Development*, Oxford: Clarendon Press.

Eckholm, E. P., (1975), *The Other Energy Crisis: Firewood*, World Watch Institute Paper No. 1, Washington DC, September 1975.

Epstein, Ms. B. and Mirow, K. R. U., (1977), *Impact on Developing Countries of Restrictive Business Practices of Transnational Corporations in the Electrical Equipment Industry: A Case Study of Brazil*, UNCTAD/ST/MD/9, New York, October, 1977.

Europe Information, (1979), 'Solar Energy: A New Area of ACP – EEC Cooperation' CEC Spokesmans Group and Directorate General for Information, Brussels.

French, D., (1978), "Renewable Energy for Africa: Needs, Opportunities, Issues", USAID, Washington.

Griffin, K., (1974), *The Political Economy of Agrarian Change: An Essay on the Green Revolution*, London: Macmillan.

Hayes, D. J., (1977), *Energy for Development: Third World Options*, World Watch Institute Paper No. 15, Washington DC, December 1977.

Hilling, D., (1976), 'Alternative Energy Sources for Africa', *African Affairs* Vol. 75, No. 300.

Hoffman, K., (1980), 'Alternative Energy Technologies and Third World Rural Energy Needs: A Case of Emerging Technological Dependency', *Development and Change*, July 1980.

Howe, J. *et al.*, (1977), *Energy for the Villages of Africa*, Overseas Development Council, Washington DC.

Newfarmer, R. S., (1978), *The International Market Power of Transnational Corporations: A Case Study of the Electrical Industry*, UNCTAD/ST/MD/13, New York.

OECD, (1979), 'Report of the Working Party of the Council to Develop a Co-ordinated Effort to help Developing Countries Bring into Use Technologies Related to Renewable Energy', Paris, May 1979.

Ramakumar, R., (1977), 'Technical and Socio-Economic Aspects of Solar Energy and Rural Development in Developing Countries', *Solar Energy*, Vol. 19 No. 6, 1977, pp. 643–650.

UNCTAD, (1978), *Energy Supplies for Developing Countries: Issues in Transfer and Development Technology*: UNCTAD Secretariat, Geneva.

Usmani, I. H., (1978). 'Power to the Villages', *Mazingira*, No. 6, 1978.

World Bank, (1975), *Rural Electrification*, Washington DC.

Statistical Appendix

Table 1   *Source of EEC imports by value and by main trading blocs, 1972, 1975–77*

	($ '000 million)				1977 value as % of world total
	1972	*1975*	*1976*	*1977*[b]	
Imports from:					
Western industrialised countries[a]	37.3	66.1	76.6	84.0	46
Developing countries	24.7	61.2	74.0	81.9	45
of which ACP	4.9	10.0	11.2	13.0	7
Centrally planned economies	6.0	11.3	13.7	15.3	8
World[a]	68.0	138.5	164.3	181.2	100

Notes: a – excluding trade between the Nine states currently in the EEC
   b – estimate

Source: Analysis of trade between the European Community and the ACP States –
   Series: Trade Flows 1979.
   (Luxembourg, Eurostat)

Table 2   *Direction of EEC exports, by value and by main trading blocs, 1972, 1975–77*

	($'000 million)				1977 value as % of world total
	1972	*1975*	*1976*	*1977*[b]	
Exports to:					
Western industrialised countries[a]	45.8	76.1	31.4	97.2	52
Developing countries	20.8	54.9	58.0	71.1	38
of which ACP	4.4	10.3	11.3	14.3	8
Centrally planned economies	6.7	16.1	15.4	16.2	9
World[a]	74.9	149.9	157.2	187.4	100

Note: a – excluding trade between the Nine states currently in the EEC
   b – estimate

Source: Analysis of trade between the European Community and the ACP States –
   Series: Trade Flows 1979.
   (Luxembourg, Eurostat)

Table 3   *EEC exports to the ACP by product group 1977*

Products	Value (Eua '000)	%
Primary products	1 762.1	14
Food, beverages & tobacco	1 228.9	10
Fuel products	389.4	3
Raw materials	143.8	1
Manufactures	10 718.0	86
Chemicals	1 228.7	10
Machinery & transport equipment	6 142.9	49
Other manufactured goods	3 346.4	27
Total EEC exports	12 503.5	100

Source: Analysis of trade between the European Community and the ACP States –
Series: Trade Flows 1979.
(Luxembourg, Eurostat)

Table 4 *EEC imports of principal products from the ACP*

Values: EUA mn
Quantity: '000 tonnes

		1973	1974	1975	1976	1977	Av annual rate of change
Crude oil							
Nigeria (85 %)*	v	991	3 917	2 890	3 103	3 216	34 %
Gabon (46 %)	q	38 684	56 167	39 806	35 721	34 392	3 %
	% of total	(16)	(37)	(33)	(30)	(26)	
Coffee							
Ivory Coast (42 %)	v	386	509	480	1 083	2 006	51 %
Kenya (56 %)	q	396	473	456	558	486.	5 %
Cameroon (36 %)	% of total	(6)	(5)	(6)	(10)	(16)	
Uganda (87 %)							
Tanzania (49 %)							

Table 4 *(continued)*

		1973	1974	1975	1976	1977	Av annual rate of change
Copper							
Zaire (41 %)	v	1031	1493	825	968	953	2 %
Zambia (92 %)	q	993	937	1035	1014	989	
Papua-New Guinea (33 %)	% of total	(7)	(14)	(10)	(9)	(8)	
Cocoa beans							
Nigeria (8 %)	v	310	489	493	584	1026	35 %
Ivory Coast (18 %)	q	465	416	394	428	387	5 %
Ghana (52 %)	% of total	(5)	(5)	(6)	(6)	(8)	
Cameroon (25 %)							
All other products	v	3453	4092	4023	4734	5 260	11 %
	% of total	(56)	(39)	(46)	(45)	(42)	
Total	v	6171	10 500	8711	10 472	12461	19 %
	% of total	(100)	(100)	(100)	(100)	(100)	

(*) Figures in brackets show share of product in total EEC imports from each country

Source: Analysis of trade between the European Community and the ACP States — Series: Trades Flows 1979 (Luxembourg, Eurostat)

Table 5 *EEC trade with the Maghreb, 1970–1978*[a] (Ecu million)

| | Tunisia | | Morocco | | Algeria | |
	Imports	Exports	Imports	Exports	Imports	Exports
1970	182.4	118.3	367.3	398.8	838.0	893.8
1971	206.6	134.4	373.4	382.5	827.5	667.6
1972	272.7	192.0	364.9	430.7	942.3	763.8
1973	341.8	191.2	498.9	581.7	1 233.4	1 069.1
1974	548.8	423.6	787.4	910.9	2 054.9	2 128.5
1975	709.8	357.3	1 045.1	805.9	2 819.8	2 049.8
1976	834.7	408.6	1 310.3	779.5	2 747.3	2 152.3
1977	977.1	552.2	1 524.3	834.3	3 674.2	2 095.9
1978	1 120.5	565.2	1 341.9	840.8	3 635.1	2 001.4

a – Total for all Nine member states.

Source: EEC Commission.

Table 6 *EEC Trade with the Mashreq 1973–8*[a] ($ million)

| | Egypt | | Lebanon | | Syria | | Jordan | |
	Imports	Exports	Imports	Exports	Imports	Exports	Imports	Exports
1973	272.1	179.9	529.4	140.6	228.5	88.5	92.6	0.1
1974	748.5	261.7	1 027.4	267.7	478.0	241.3	140.7	0.2
1975	1 330.9	166.1	847.6	75.2	658.5	441.5	240.2	6.1
1976	1 413.0	330.5	180.2	48.8	789.7	518.5	382.9	7.6
1977	1 764.3	423.1	750.6	43.6	1 014.4	496.9	479.5	2.8
1978	2 559.6	1 135.6	847.1	41.3	901.3	518.9	529.0	8.4

a – Total for all Nine member states.

Source: EEC Commission.

Table 7 *Commitments of financial assistance under the Lomé Convention up to end 1979, by method of financing and administering organisation* (in Ecu million)

	Administered by EEC Commission		Administered by EIB		Total	
	value	%	value	%	value	%
EDF Resources	2 121.9	100	119.4	30.5	2 241.3	89.2
– Grants	1 475.8	69.5	42.6	10.9	1 518.4	60.4
of which: interest						
· rate subsidies	–	–	42.6	10.9	42.6	1.7
exceptional aid	110.9	5.2	–	–	110.9	4.4
– Special loans	324.1	15.3	–	–	324.1	12.9
– Risk capital	–	–	76.8[a]	19.6	76.8[a]	3.1
– Stabex	322.0	15.2	–	–	322.0	12.8
EIB Resources						
– Loans	–	–	272.6	69.5	272.6	10.8
Total	2 121.9	100	392.0	100	2 513.9	100

Note: a – including Ecu 2 million pending utilisation from the overall authorisation for studies.

Source: EEC Commission.

Table 8 *Sectoral distribution of commitments from EDF IV to ACP, up to 31 January 1980*

Sector	Amount Ecu '000	%
Development of Production	851 932	38
Industrial development	320 145	
Tourism	5 335	
Rural production	526 452	
Transport & Communications infrastructure	460 042	21
Social Development	332 076	15
Education & training	203 098	
Health	45 219	
Water engineering, housing & urban infrastructure	83 759	
Trade Promotion	32 176	1
Exceptional Aid	113 922	5
Stabex	305 026	14
Miscellaneous	131 804	6

Source: EEC Commission.

Table 9   *Stabex transfers to ACP and OCT, 1975–79, by country*

Recipient	1979 Eua '000	1975–79 Eua '000	%
Belize	–	342.4	–
Benin	349.3	20 366.7	5
Burundi	–	1 485.7	–
Cameroon	–	4 065.0	1
Cape Verde	429.4	1 206.6	–
CAR	3 847.0	7 829.6	2
Chad	2 664.6	7 336.2	2
Comoros	431.2	2 326.4	1
Congo	–	7 361.7	2
Djibouti	–	691.9	–
Dominica	2 892.9	2 892.9	1
Ethiopia	–	14 420.1	4
Fiji	–	2 115.0	1
Gabon	–	6 703.3	2
Gambia	5 026.1	7 514.8	2
Ghana	–	5 176.4	1
Guinea Bissau	2 480.5	11 288.3	3
Ivory Coast	–	15 000.0	4
Kiribati	–	2 283.4	1
Liberia	–	7 586.9	2
Madagascar	2 845.1	5 747.5	2
Mali	3 894.2	9 780.9	3
Mauritania	–	37 000.5	10
New Hebrides	–	1 430.9	–
Niger	–	22 654.0	6
Rwanda	–	608.8	–
Senegal	–	65 106.4	17
Sierra Leone	–	3 977.3	1
Solomon Islands	–	2 173.4	1
Somalia	–	1 932.1	–
Sudan[a]	27 190.1	39 143.5	10
Swaziland	4 365.5	13 224.9	3
Tanzania	–	20 701.6	5
Togo	–	3 626.6	1
Tonga	58.6	1 208.0	–
Tuvalu	–	174.7	–
Uganda	6 900.3	20 595.5	5
Upper Volta	–	7 261.9	2
Western Samoa	–	2 837.5	1
Total	63 374.8	387 178.7	

a – Does not include a small payment for sesame seed in 1979.

Columns may not add up due to rounding.

Source: EEC Commission

Table 10 *Stabex transfers to ACP and OCT, 1975–79, by commodity*

Commodity	1979 Eua '000	1975–79 Eua '000	%
Groundnuts	33 564.8	71 338.8	18
Groundnut oil	3 999.9	68 021.5	18
Groundnut Cake	1 026.1	17 594.6	5
Iron Ore	4 365.5	61 789.5	16
Cotton	10 667.7	43 359.4	11
Rough Timber	–	38 953.1	10
Sawn Timber	–	1 039.0	–
Sisal	–	20 577.4	5
Coffee	–	14 494.3	4
Copra	–	8 456.3	2
Raw Hides, Skins & Leather	–	9 093.8	2
Bananas	3 322.3	5 813.4	2
Tea	3 093.5	8 376.3	2
Cloves	431.2	2 303.5	1
Vanilla	2 903.7	2 903.7	1
Palm Nut Oil	–	5 567.2	1
Palm Oil	–	2 232.9	–
Cocoa	–	1 057.6	–
Cocoa Paste	–	463.6	–
Coconut Oil	–	2 115.0	–
Gum Arabic	–	848.5	–
Pyrethrum	–	608.8	–
Ylang-Ylang	–	170.6	–
	63 374.7	387 178.7	

Notes: Columns may not add up due to rounding.
At July 1980 a small payment in respect of sesame seeds was still being processed.

Source: EEC Commission.

Table 11 *Commitments and Disbursements from EDF IV*

Commitments as at 31 January 1980; disbursements as at 30 November 1979 (in Ecu '000)

Recipient	Grants	Special loans	Stabex	Commitments Exceptional aid	EIB interest subsidy	EIB risk capital	Total	Disbursements Total
ACP								
Bahamas	716	690	0	0	0	0	1 406	326
Barbados	2 329	1 598	0	0	364	0	4 291	2 001
Benin	30 906	350	20 017	20	0	0	51 293	22 385
Botswana	18 849	650	0	2 670	0	0	22 169	5 668
Burundi	37 258	2 960	1 486	2 059	0	500	44 263	15 891
Cameroon	25 039	17 457	4 065	0	4 680	2 300	53 541	26 141
Cape Verde	2 239	0	778	1 350	0	80	4 447	1 490
C.A.R.	29 182	535	3 983	950	0	0	34 650	9 510
Chad	33 307	7 550	0	300	0	7 500	48 657	24 614
Comoros	6 519	0	1 896	2 597	0	0	11 012	4 525
Congo	18 687	3 846	7 362	250	0	3 150	33 295	23 914
Djibouti	2 995	0	692	0	0	1 000	4 687	1 420
Dominique	2 284	0	2 480	3 300	0	0	8 064	2 300
Equatorial Guinea	431	0	0	300	0	0	731	6
Ethiopia	80 447	0	14 420	2 750	0	0	97 617	27 622
Fiji	2 929	6 674	2 115	2 500	2 098	0	16 316	6 186
Gabon	2 132	7 057	6 703	0	0	0	15 892	10 821
Gambia	10 194	0	2 489	749	0	0	13 432	5 066
Ghana	22 494	19 570	5 176	2 430	2 433	0	52 103	16 165
Grenada	2 009	0	0	0	0	0	2 009	199
Guinea	35 356	20 000	0	3 035	0	0	58 391	11 366

Table 11 (continued)

Recipient	Commitments							Disbursements
	Grants	Special loans	Stabex	Exceptional aid	EIB interest subsidy	EIB risk capital	Total	Total
Guinea Bissau	16 896	0	8 808	467	0	0	26 171	16 612
Guyana	6 891	6 372	0	0	0	3 200	16 463	2 729
Ivory Coast	12 973	22 991	15 000	0	5 945	948	57 857	29 632
Jamaica	10 534	8 627	0	275	0	0	19 436	6 099
Kiribati	170	0	2 283	0	0	0	2 453	2 283
Kenya	34 285	36 958	0	300	7 800	1 166	80 509	27 574
Lesotho	18 524	0	0	1 230	0	0	19 754	4 676
Liberia	20 026	4 800	7 587	0	1 242	286	33 941	5 872
Madagascar	40 995	0	2 903	1 700	0	1 190	46 788	14 228
Malawi	50 644	8 500	0	4 000	1 410	987	65 541	17 999
Mali	67 398	1 220	5 887	1 020	0	3 650	79 175	34 807
Mauritius	4 071	4 600	0	3 700	886	0	13 257	4 921
Mauretania	20 881	0	37 001	1 307	3 637	0	62 826	49 377
Niger	62 178	0	22 654	9 614	1 047	900	96 393	63 776
Nigeria	4 395	0	0	0	3 040	0	7 435	3 953
Papua New Guinea	1 939	0	0	0	1 235	1 600	4 774	3 912
Rwanda	55 567	2 564	609	6 435	0	3 000	68 175	28 033
Saint Lucia	2 305	0	0	0	0	0	2 305	1 026
Sao Tomé	1 673	0	0	300	0	0	1 973	261
Senegal	39 951	15 313	65 106	3 685	0	200	124 255	90 814
Seychelles	2 002	0	0	0	0	620	2 622	696
Sierra Leone	25 906	1 000	3 977	0	0	0	30 883	8 494
Solomon Islands	1 455	0	2 173	0	0	0	3 628	2 257
Somalia	34 611	0	1 932	3 426	0	0	39 969	14 424

Table 11 (continued)

Recipient	Commitments							Disbursements
	Grants	Special loans	Stabex	Exceptional aid	EIB interest subsidy	EIB risk capital	Total	Total
ACP								
Sudan	54 209	9 000	2 628	1 536	0	6 500	73 873	17 661
Suriname	5 645	2 000	0	0	0	0	7 645	1 118
Swaziland	8 853	3 500	3 369	0	1 626	153	17 501	9 713
Tanzania	53 402	21 950	20 702	355	741	7 400	104 550	43 397
Togo	32 332	0	3 626	0	419	3 250	39 627	22 680
Tonga	2 865	130	1 149	200	0	0	4 344	2 475
Trinidad & Tobago	4 234	2 890	0	0	1 577	0	8 701	2 305
Tuvalu	0	0	175	0	0	0	175	175
Uganda	23 958	0	13 695	500	0	0	38 180	15 764
Upper Volta	43 059	0	7 262	0	0	4 428	54 749	33 376
Western Samoa	3 699	890	2 838	0	0	0	7 427	3 850
Zaire	77 950	8 033	0	19 300	0	5 230	110 513	26 656
Zambia	23 296	17 595	0	17 012	411	632	58 946	22 033
Total	1 236 101	267 870	305 026	101 622	40 591	59 870	2 011 080	853 274
Regional projects	122 239	57 700	0	0	2 699	6 000	188 638	57 393
DOM/TOM	19 710	8 631	1 773	0	0	1 000	31 114	8 462
Grand Total	1 403 727	334 201	306 799	113 922	43 290	68 943	2 270 882	939 850

Source: EEC Commission

Table 12 *Breakdown of EDF IV funded contracts according to nationality of suppliers, up to 31 December 1979*

Country of firm	% share of: Works contracts	Supply contracts	Technical co-operation contracts	All contracts
Belgium	5.3	5.1	9.5	6.1
Denmark	0.5	0.03	2.9	0.9
France	24.3	21.1	19.5	22.7
Germany	6.9	21.4	20.1	12.5
Ireland	0	0	1.6	0.3
Italy	11.6	21.1	11.8	13.6
Luxembourg	0	0	1.9	0.4
Netherlands	4.5	4.3	7.8	5.1
United Kingdom	3.7	13.3	10.5	7.0
Total EEC	56.8	86.33	85.6	68.6
ACP and TOM	42.2	10.0	14.4	30.1
Third Countries	0.9	3.8	0	1.3
Total in Ecu '000	516 763	179 173	172 939	868 875

Note: columns may not add up due to rounding.

Source: EEC Commission.

Table 13 *EIB lending to the ACP, Maghreb and Mashreq in 1979 (in Eua million)*

Recipient	From EIB own resources		Special section operations	
	No. of projects	Amount	No. of projects	Amount
Maghreb	3	50.0	1	14.0
Morocco	1	26.0	1	14.0
Tunisia	2	24.0	0	0
Mashreq	8	108.7	2	3.8
Egypt	3	65.0	0	0
Jordan	2	11.0	1	0.3
Lebanon	2	17.0	0	0
Syria	1	15.7	1	3.5
Africa	10	70.7	12	13.1
Cape Verde	0	0	1	0.1
Ivory Coast	3	15.8	1	0.5
Gambia	0	0	1	2.3
Ghana	1	6.0	0	0
Mali	0	0	1	2.5
Mauretania	1	25.0	0	0
Niger	1	4.5	0	0
Senegal	0	0	2	1.5
Burundi	0	0	1	0.5
Cameroon	3	14.4	1	2.3
Djibouti	0	0	1	1.0
Kenya	1	5.0	0	0
Madagascar	0	0	2	2.3
Swaziland	0	0	1	0.1
Caribbean	1	2.5	1	0.1
Barbados	1	2.5	0	0
Jamaica	0	0	1	0.1
Total	22	231.9	16	31.0

Source: EIB *Annual Report 1979* (Luxembourg).

Documentary Appendix

Extracts from the Second Lomé Convention

- Protocol No. 3 on ACP Sugar
- Title 3 Chapter 1 on aid to mineral projects
- Article 76 on energy aid
- Annex XV on treatment of migrant workers
- Article 64, Annex IX and an exchange of letters between the President of the EEC Council and the President of the ACP Council of Ministers, concerning investment codes.

Protocol No 3

on ACP sugar

Article 1

1. The Community undertakes for an indefinite period to purchase and import, at guaranteed prices, specific quantities of cane sugar, raw or white, which originate in the ACP States and which these States undertake to deliver to it.

2. The safeguard clause in Article 10 of the Convention shall not apply. The implementation of this Protocol is carried out within the framework of the management of the common organization of the sugar market which, however, shall no way prejudice the commitment of the Community under paragraph 1.

Article 2

1. Without prejudice to Article 7, no change in this Protocol may enter into force until a period of five years has elapsed from the date on which the Convention enters into force. Thereafter, such changes as may be agreed upon will come into force at a time to be agreed.

2. The conditions for implementing the guarantee referred to in Article 1 shall be re-examined before the end of the seventh year of their application.

Article 3

1. Quantities of cane sugar referred to in Article 1, expressed in metric tons of white sugar, hereinafter referred to as "agreed quantities", for delivery in each 12-month period referred to in Article (1), shall be as follows:

Barbados	49 300
Fiji	163 600
Guyana	157 700
Jamaica	118 300
Kenya	5 000
Madagascar	10 000
Malawi	20 000

Mauritius	487 200
People's Republic of the Congo	10 000
Swaziland	116 400
Tanzania	10 000
Trinidad and Tobago	69 000
Uganda	5 000

2. Subject to Article 7, these quantities cannot be reduced without the consent of the individual States concerned.

3. Nevertheless, in respect of the period up to 30 June 1975, the agreed quantities, expressed in metric tons of white sugar, shall be as follows:

Barbados	29 600
Fiji	25 600
Guyana	29 600
Jamaica	83 800
Madagascar	2 000
Mauritius	65 300
Swaziland	19 700
Trinidad and Tobago	54 200

Article 4

1. In each 12-month period from 1 July to 30 June inclusive, hereinafter referred to as the "delivery period", the sugar-exporting ACP States undertake to deliver the quantities referred to in Article 3(1), subject to any adjustments resulting from the application of Article 7. A similar undertaking shall apply equally to the quantities referred to in Article 3 (3) in respect of the period up to 30 June 1975, which shall also be regarded as a delivery period.

2. The quantities to be delivered up to 30 June 1975, referred to in Article 3(3), shall include supply en route from port of shipment or, in the case of landlocked States across frontier.

3. Deliveries of ACP cane sugar in the period up to 30 June 1975 shall benefit from the guaranteed prices applicable in the delivery period beginning 1 July 1975. Identical arrangements may be made for subsequent delivery periods.

Article 5

1. White or raw sugar shall be marketed on the Community market at prices freely negotiated between buyers and sellers.

2. The Community shall not intervene if and when a Member State allows selling prices within its borders to exceed the Community's threshold price.

3. The Community undertakes to purchase, at the guaranteed price, quantities of white or raw sugar, within agreed quantities, which cannot be marketed in the Community at a price equivalent to or in excess of the guaranteed price.

4. The guaranteed price, expressed in units of account, shall refer to unpacked sugar, cif European ports of the Community, and shall be fixed in respect of standard quality sugar. It shall be negotiated annually, within the price range of obtaining in the Community, taking into account all relevant economic factors, and shall be decided at the latest by 1 May immediately preceding the delivery period to which it will apply.

Article 6

Purchase at the guaranteed price, referred to in Article 5(3), shall be assured through the medium of the intervention agencies or of other agents appointed by the Community.

Article 7

1. If, during any delivery period, a sugar-exporting ACP State fails to deliver its agreed quantity in full for reasons of force majeure the Commission shall, at the request of the State concerned, allow the necessary additional period for delivery.

2. If a sugar-exporting ACP State informs the Commission during the course of a delivery period that it will be unable to deliver its agreed quantity in full and that it does not wish to have the additional period referred to in paragraph 1, the shortfall shall be reallocated by the Commission for delivery during the delivery period in question. Such re-allocation shall be made by the Commission after consultation with the States s concerned.

3. If, during any delivery period, a sugar-exporting ACP State fails to deliver its agreed quantity in full for reasons other than force majeure, that quantity shall be reduced in respect of each subsequent delivery period by the undelivered quantity.

4. It may be decided by the Commission that in respect of subsequent delivery periods, the undelivered quantity shall be reallocated between the other States which are referred to in Article 3. Such re-allocation shall be made in consultation with the States concerned.

Article 8

1. At the request of one or more of the States supplying sugar under the terms of this Protocol, or of the Community, consultations relating to all measures necessary for the application of this Protocol shall take place within an appropriate institutional framework to be adopted by the Contracting Parties. For this purpose the institutions established by the Convention may be used during the period of application of the Convention.

2. In the event of the Convention ceasing to be operative, the sugar supplying States referred to in paragraph 1 and the Community shall adopt the appropriate institutional provisions to ensure the continued application of the provisions of this Protocol.

3. The periodical reviews provided for under this Protocol shall take place within the agreed institutional framework.

Article 9

Special types of sugar traditionally delivered to Member States by certain sugar-exporting ACP States shall be included in, and treated on the same basis as, the quantities referred to in Article 3.

Article 10

The provisions of this protocol shall remain in force after the date specified in Article 91 of the Convention. After that date the Protocol may be denounced by the Community with respect to each ACP State and by each ACP State with respect to the Community, subject to two years' notice.

Annex

Declarations on Protocol No 3 to the ACP-EEC Convention of Lomé

1. Joint declaration concerning possible requests for participation in the provisions of Protocol No 3

Any request from an ACP State Contracting Party to the Convention not specifically referred to in Protocol No 3 to participate in the provisions of that Protocol shall be examined([1]).

2. Declaration by the Community concerning sugar originating in Belize, St-Kitts-Nevis-Anguilla and Surinam

(a) The Community undertakes to adopt the necessary measures to ensure the same treatment as provided for in Protocol No 3, for the following quantities of cane sugar, raw or white, originating in:
Belize: 39 400 metric tons;
St-Kitts-Nevis-Anguilla: 14 800 metric tons;
Surinam: 4 000 metric tons.

(b) Nevertheless, in respect of the period up to 30 June 1975, the quantities shall be as follows:
Belize: 14,800 metric tons;
St.-Kitts-Nevis-Anguilla: 7,900 metric tons([2]).

3. Declarations by the Community on Article 10 of Protocol No 3

The Community declares that Article 10 of Protocol No 3 providing for the possibility of denunciation in that Protocol, under the conditions set out in that Article, is for the purposes of juridical security and does not represent for the Community any qualification or limitation of the principles enunciated in Article 1 of that Protocol ([3]).

Title III
Mineral Products

Chapter 1

Project and programme aid

Article 49

With a view to contributing towards the creation of a more solid basis for the development of the ACP States whose economies are largely dependent on the mining sectors and in particular towards helping them cope with a decline in their capacity to export mining products to the Community and the corresponding decline in their export earnings, a system shall be established to assist these States in their efforts to remedy the harmful effects on their income of serious temporary disruptions affecting those mining sectors and beyond the control of the ACP States concerned.

Article 50

The system laid down in Article 49 shall apply to the following products:
- copper, including associated production of cobalt;
- phosphates;
- manganese;
- bauxite and alumina;
- tin;
- roasted iron pyrites and iron ore, whether or not in agglomerate form (including pellets), excluding, during the period mentioned in Article 25(2), the cases referred to in that Article.

If, not sooner than twelve months following the entry into force of this Convention, one or more products not contained in the above list, but upon which the economies of one or more ACP States depend to a considerable extent, are affected by serious disturbance, the Council of Ministers shall decide, not later than six months after the presentation of a request by the ACP State or States concerned, whether or not to include the said product or products in the list.

Article 51

For the purpose specified in Article 49, and for the period of application of this Convention, a special financing facility shall be set up to which the Community shall allocate an overall amount of 280 million EUA to cover all its commitments under this system:

(1) This amount shall be managed by the Commission.

(2) This overall amount shall be divided into a number of equal annual instalments corresponding to the number of years of application. Each year, except the last, the Council of Ministers, on the basis of a report submitted to it by the Commission, may authorize, where required, a maximum of 50% of the following year's instalment to be used in advance.

(3) Whatever balance remains at the end of each year of application of this Convention, except the last, shall be carried over automatically to the following year.

(4) If the resources available for any year of application are insufficient, the amounts due shall be reduced accordingly.

(5) The resources available for each year of application shall be made up of the following elements:

– the annual instalment, reduced by any amounts used under (2) above;

– the sums carried over under (3) above.

Before the expiry of the period referred to in Article 188, the Council of Ministers shall decide on the allocation of any balances remaining from the overall amount referred to in this Article.

Article 52

Possible recourse to the means of financing available under the special facility provided for in Article 51 shall be open to the countries eligible under Article 53 when, for a product covered by Article 50 and exported to the Community, a substantial fall is recorded, or can be expected over the following months, in their capacity to produce, or to export, or in their export earnings to such an extent as to seriously affect the development policy of the ACP State concerned by seriously compromising the profitability of an otherwise viable and economic line of production, thus preventing it from renewing at a normal rate or maintaining the production plant or export capacity.

The possible recourse referred to above shall also be available when a substantial fall in the production or export capacity is experienced, or is foreseen, owing to accidents and serious technical mishaps or grave political events, whether internal or external.

A substantial fall in production or export capacity shall be taken to mean 10%.

Article 53

An ACP State which, during the preceding four years, has, as a general rule, derived at least 15% of its export earnings from a product covered by Article 50 may apply for financial aid from the resources allocated to the special financing facility if the conditions laid down in Article 52 are fulfilled.

However, for the States listed in Article 155(3), the figure stipulated in the first paragraph shall be 10%.

The application for aid shall be made to the Commission which shall examine it in conjunction with the ACP State concerned. The fact that the conditions have been fulfilled shall be established by common accord between the Community and the ACP State. Notification thereof by the Commission to the ACP State shall entitle the latter to Community aid from the special financing facility.

Article 54

The aid referred to in Article 53 shall be directed to the objectives defined in Article 49.

The amount of this aid to finance projects or programmes shall be determined by the Commission in the light of the funds available under the special financing facility, the nature of the projects or programmes proposed by the ACP States concerned and the possibilities for co-financing. In determining the amount, account shall be taken of the scale of the reduction in production or export capacity and of the losses of earnings suffered by the ACP States and corresponding to those identified in Article 52.

Under no circumstances may a single ACP State be eligible for more than 50% of the funds available under an annual instalment.

The procedures applicable to assistance in the above circumstances and the implementing arrangements shall be as provided for under Title VII; they shall take account of the need for rapid implementation of the aid.

Article 55

To permit the implementation of precautionary measures to halt deterioration of production plant during the appraisal or implementation of these projects or programmes, the Community may grant an advance to any ACP State which so requests. This possibility shall not exclude recourse by the ACP State concerned to the emergency aid provided for in Article 137.

Since an advance is granted as a means of prefinancing projects or programmes which it precedes or to which it is preparatory, account shall be taken of the importance and nature of those projects or programmes when the amount of the advance is fixed.

The advance shall take the form of supplies or of the provision of services, or of cash payments if this arrangement is considered more appropriate.

It shall be incorporated in the amount earmarked for Community operations in the form of projects or programmes at the time when the financing agreement relating to such operations is signed.

Article 56

Aid granted from the special financing facility shall be reimbursed on the same terms and conditions as special loans account being taken of the provisions adopted in favour of the States listed in Article 155(3).

Energy

Article 76

1. The Community and the ACP States recognize the mutual benefits of co-operation in the field of *energy*. With a view to developing the conventional and non-conventional energy potential and the self-sufficiency of the ACP States, the Community will assist, inter alia, in the following areas:

(a) preparation of inventories on energy resources and demand, adequate attention being paid to non-commercial energy demand;

(b) implementation of alternative energy strategies in programmes and projects that will take special account of the experience of the ACP States and cover inter alia wind, solar, geothermal and hydro-energy sources;

(c) development of the investment potential for the exploration and development of national and regional energy sources as well as the development of sites of exceptional energy production enabling the establishment of energy-intensive industry;

(d) strengthening of the management and control of the ACP States of their energy resources in terms of their development objectives by all the means provided for in this Convention;

(e) establishment of a rural energy programme with emphasis on rural energy technologies and energy planning that can meet basic needs;

(f) promotion of research, adaptation and dissemination of appropriate technology as well as the training needed to meet energy-related manpower needs;

(g) production in the ACP States of equipment for the production and distribution of energy as well as the application of energy-saving techniques;

(h) implementation of measures that will minimize the negative impact of energy production on the environment as well as promote environmentally positive projects;

(i) conservation of existing and future energy resources of the ACP States, whether conventional or non-conventional.

2. Programmes, projects or schemes undertaken in the field of energy co-operation and involving Community financing shall be implemented in accordance with Title VII.

In relation to research and experimental projects as well as exploration and development projects of mutual interest, the resources provided for under Title VII may be supplemented by:

(1) other Community financial and technical resources;

(2) actions aimed at the mobilization of public and private capital, notably co-financing.

Annex XV

Joint declaration on workers who are nationals of one of the Contracting Parties and are residing legally in the territory of a Member State or an ACP State

1. Each Member State shall accord to workers who are nationals of an ACP State legally employed in its territory treatment free from any discrimination based on nationality, as regards working conditions and pay, in relation to its own nationals.

Each ACP State shall accord the same treatment to workers who are nationals of the Member States legally employed on its territory.

2. Workers who are nationals of an ACP State legally employed in the territory of a Member State and members of their families living with them shall, as regards social security benefits linked to employment, in that Member State enjoy treatment free from any discrimination based on nationality in relation to nationals of that Member State.

Each ACP State shall accord to workers who are nationals of Member States and legally employed in its territory, and to members of their families, treatment similar to that laid down in paragraph 1.

3. These provisions shall not affect any rights or obligations arising from bilateral agreements binding the ACP States and the Member States where those agreements provide for more favourable treatment for nationals of the ACP States or of the Member States.

4. The Parties hereto agree that the matters referred to in this Declaration shall be resolved satisfactorily and, if necessary, through bilateral negotiations with a view to concluding appropriate agreements.

Investment Codes

Article 64

The Contracting Parties agree that the treatment of investment coming from Member States to the ACP States shall be governed by the provisions of the joint declaration contained in Annex IX of the Final Act.

Annex IX

Joint declaration on investments relating to Article 64 of the Convention

1. Where an ACP State has entered, or enters, into an inter-governmental agreement relating to the treatment of investments with any Member States, the ACP State concerned recognizes that the right of non-discriminatory treatment of investments coming from Member States of the Community in ACP States takes effect from the entry into force of the Convention.

2. (a) The application of this right shall be based on bilateral inter-governmental investment agreements which shall serve as reference agreements.

(b) As regards such bilateral inter-governmental investment agreements concluded before the entry into force of this Convention, the application of non-discriminatory treatment shall take into account any provisions in the reference agreement. The ACP State shall have the right to modify or adapt this treatment when international obligations and/or changed de facto circumstances so necessitate.

3. For the purpose of applying non-discriminatory treatment on the basis of paragraph 2(a) the Contracting States shall proceed to bilateral inter-governmental Exchanges of Letters or other appropriate from required by law of a Contracting State.

4. Any Contracting State has the right to ask for such an agreement. The agreement when concluded shall come into effect without delay in accordance with the law of the ACP State concerned.

5. Such agreements shall cover disputes relating to investment arising only after the entry into force of the new Convention.

6. The treatment of investments made before the entry into force of this Convention shall be examined by the two parties in the light of the provisions of the agreement of reference.

LETTER FROM PRESIDENT O'KENNEDY TO PRESIDENT ST. JOHN (31st OCTOBER 1979)

Dear President St. John,

Following on my statement to the ACP Council this morning, I now wish, as agreed at that meeting, to convey formally to you the following understanding:

1. Wherever the word "right" is used, in the Annex to Article 64 of the Convention, it is synonymous with the word "principle";

2. The right or principle thus referred to in paragraphs 1 and 2(a) of the Annex can not take automatic effect, but can only come into effect through the bilateral inter-governmental agreement referred to in paragraph 3;

3. The application of such right or principle does not purport to, and can not in fact, infringe the sovereignty of any Member State party to the Convention;

4. The reference in paragraph 2(b) to "any provisions" of the reference agreement covers obligations which the EEC Government concerned must assume in the bilateral agreement to be concluded;

5. Finally, I confirm that as provided for in, and subject to, paragraphs 5 and 6 of the Annex, retroactivity is not implied as a general principle.

                              Yours faithfully,

                              Michael O'KENNEDY

LETTER FROM PRESIDENT ST. JOHN TO PRESIDENT O'KENNEDY
(1st NOVEMBER 1979)

Dear President O'Kennedy,

        I acknowledge receipt of your undermentioned letter:

'Dear President St. John,

Following on my statement to the ACP Council this morning, I now wish, as agreed at that meeting, to convey formally to you the following understanding:

1. Wherever the word "right" is used, in the Annex to Article 64 of the Convention, it is synonymous with the word "principle";

2. The right or principle thus referred to in paragraphs 1 and 2(a) of the Annex can not take automatic effect, but can only come into effect through the bilateral inter-governmental agreement referred to in paragraph 3;

3. The application of such right or principle does not purport to, and can not in fact, infringe the sovereignty of any Member State party to the Convention;

4. The reference in paragraph 2(b) to "any provisions" of the reference agreement covers obligations which the EEC Government concerned must assume in the bilateral agreement to be concluded;

5. Finally, I confirm that as provided for in, and subject to, paragraphs 5 and 6 of the Annex, retroactivity is not implied as a general principle.

Yours faithfully,

Michael O'KENNEDY'

My understanding of your letter is that wherever the word 'right' is used in the Annex to Article 64 of the Convention it is synonymous with the word

'principle' save in paragraphs 2(b) and 4, of the Annex.

Finally, I confirm that, save as may be provided for in and subject to paragraphs 5 and 6 of the Annex, retroactivity is not implied.

In conclusion, I must ask you to confirm our understanding that this correspondence would be incorporated in the minutes of the signing of the Convention.

Yours truly,

H.B. St. John

Index